Felipe Gómez A.

Attitude-E

Felipe Gómez A.

Attitude-E

The Method for Being Entrepreneurial and Fulfilling your Dreams

Actitude-E
© 2015, Felipe Gómez Arbeláez

Edition and design
Intermedio Editores
Diagramming
Pablo Burgos
Cover design
Lisandro Moreno Rojas
© Intermedio Editores SAS

First edition in Spanish, March 2015
This book may not be reproduced
without the written permission of the author.

Bookings:
felipe.gomez@me.com
www.felipegomeza.co
@actitude

A B C D E F G H I J
Stampato in Colombia - *Printed in Colombia*

For Pili, the love of my life.
Infinite thanks:
For focusing my dreams.
For giving me energy through your love,
dedication, and support.
For your determination to love God.
For being the best teammate in my life.
For the elasticity of your mind that always questions,
digs deeper, proposes, and raises the bar.
For your unconditional engagement with our family and,
especially, with our children.
For being my star and for the brightness of your presence.

Table of Contents

Introduction

At this moment, I feel honored knowing you have my book in your hands. I don't know if it was the cover that caught your attention, if someone gave it to you, or if a friend, relative or colleague recommended it. Whichever the case, I would personally like to thank you for your interest and your trust. This is my first book and, I must admit, that writing it was more difficult than I thought, but it really did prove to be an edifying exercise and a real entrepreneurial endeavor.

The idea of writing this book came up from the reaction of many people who, after listening to one of my presentations on the topic, asked me: "Do you have a book?" When I told them that I didn't, they responded with a strange mix of frustration and enthusiasm, finally telling me that I "have to write one!" While initially some personal and professional situations made me postpone the task, I finally had the courage to sit down and write. This is the result of that effort and I feel pleased to share it with you with all the love and humility that went into it.

I sincerely hope that it will help you reflect on your life and help you to understand the immense power of entrepreneurship.

I know, with certainty, that you have many dreams in your life that you want to achieve. Some are probably focused on personal growth while others serve to form, strengthen, or sustain a family. There are also dreams that can help advance your work, start your own business, enhance your capacity to help others, or to grow spiritually (whatever the belief or credo).

I can also imagine that there is a constant internal struggle between the desire to realize those dreams and the fear of risk and failure in working on them. All these factors determine how many of these dreams will come to fruition and how many will remain in a stage of imagining, leaving us with a shadow of what they could have become.

This book is based on my life experience and in the study and analyses of great men and women who were able to turn their dreams into reality. I hope these examples will be a source of inspiration so you can do the same with yours. As the author, I seek to accompany you in this process. My aim is to help kindle and expand the entrepreneurial fire within you. It is a state of mind that is bigger and more powerful than you think. It is your duty – and mine also – not only to awaken that fire, as I mentioned, but to harness it, because only by leveraging it, will you be able to maximize your potential for being, growing, doing, and loving.

In his famous commencement address at Stanford University, Apple founder Steve Jobs explained how we can better understand the events – good and bad – in our lives as time goes on by "connecting the dots" to better understand why things happen to us. In my case, in connecting the dots, I arrived at two events that occurred when I was still a child where I discovered the power of dreams and turning them into reality. Although these dreams were childish, perhaps even trivial, they taught me a great lesson that, looking back, has been very influential in my life.

The first event happened when I was in the seventh grade in school and we were assigned a book by Gabriel Garcia Marquez, later a Nobel Prize winner in literature, entitled Story of a Shipwrecked Sailor. It is a journalistic report that tells the real-life story of Luis Alejandro Velasco, who managed to survive for ten days after being shipwrecked at sea. His ship, the ARC Caldas, sank in the Atlantic Ocean in February of 1955. I remember the feelings and interest I had while reading the story, my inability to put the book down, and the many feelings I had while reading it.

When I finished the book, I was left with many unanswered questions and a desire to seek out the person that could answer them. So, I sought out Luis Alejandro Velasco, who "was proclaimed as a national hero, kissed by beauty queens, and made rich by publicity, and then rejected by the government and forgotten forever."

It had been almost 30 years after the shipwreck and about 15 years after the book was published. I didn't know if Velasco was still alive or in what country or city he might reside, but I longed to meet him and though it seemed like a fool's errand, I wanted to hear firsthand his side of the story.

Of course, I started the search when there was no Google or Facebook. I was armed only with the white pages. So, with curiosity and a steadfast resolve, I looked for the letter V to find the Velasco last name, and, in refining my search, I found about twenty-five entries of Luis Alejandro Velasco residing in the city of Bogota.

I picked up the phone and started calling them, one by one, asking with the innocent voice of a boy if the Luis Alejandro who lived there was the hero I was looking for. The first twenty calls were unsuccessful. They made fun of me, or hung up, or just told me that it wasn't the person I was asking for. I kept trying without losing hope and, in one of the last calls – I don't recall if it was the twenty-second or twenty-fourth call – a woman answered and was silent for a few seconds after my question. The silence, to me, felt like an eternity, but, finally she said: "Yes, Luis Alejandro Velasco, the person in the book, lives here. But he is not here right now. Who is calling?" I was a bundle of nerves and could hardly breathe. I told her the story and why I wanted to meet him. Somehow, I convinced her and she told me to call back in an hour.

I called back and he answered. He genuinely listened and answered my questions with kindness and humility. I remember that he was excited about the call, even grateful. We spoke for a time and I decided to invite him to my school to tell us his side of the story first-hand. To my astonishment, he warmly accepted. The next day, I enthusiastically told my Spanish teacher the story and in spite of my intensity and enthusiasm, she didn't actually believe a word I said. We were walking side by side and I assured her: "I swear, Miss! It's true... I swear!" In pleading my case, and focusing my attention on conveying the sincerity of my words, I ran into a post and my forehead began to bleed. She said, "All right, Felipe... I believe you!"

After sorting out the details and making final arrangements, Luis Alejandro Velasco visited my school. In a large auditorium, he shared his experiences with a group of students and teachers who sat listening intently to his tale. And that, dear reader, is how we got to know the protagonist of Marquez's great book. We discovered many details that were omitted from the published story and enjoyed the magic of a great storyteller told by the person who lived it.

I learned that even with a bruised ego and bloodied forehead a dream stoutly pursued can come true!

The second event occurred a few years later, when my parents took me to a Magic Festival in a small theater in Bogota called the "House of Spain". The event, organized by the Colombian magician Gustavo Lorgia, included several extraordinary magicians. I remember that each of their respective shows fascinated me and got me excited about the art of magic. When the show ended, I was left stunned, with my mouth agape and my heart racing. I wanted to learn the secrets of what I witnessed; I wanted to learn magic.

I got home that evening. It was late and I tried to sleep, but in tossing and turning I kept wondering how Jose Luis Ballesteros had managed to predict the card I was thinking about, or how Juan Tamariz conjured a handkerchief that a person in the audience had cut to pieces, or how Pepe Carrol had made a shuffled card deck appear in sequential order with the power of his mind.

I was so restless, I got up and sought out a familiar friend, the white pages, and I looked up Gustavo Lorgia's phone number. This time though, I fortunately only found one person under that name.

The next day, after arriving home from school, I called him and he answered. I told him that I had been at the magic show the day before and that I wanted to learn magic. I asked him if he could teach me. He politely, but hurriedly, told me that he didn't teach and suggested that I look elsewhere. He said good-bye and hung up the phone. I was frustrated but undeterred. The next day, I returned home from school and tried calling again, but my pleas were met with the same answer.

After that day, I would call him every day when I arrived home from school, until one day, after a couple of weeks of this daily routine, he asked to put one of my parents on the phone. I was excited, thinking that he was finally going to relent and accept me as a pupil. My father came to the phone and heard a voice that said – or perhaps begged – "Please ask your son to stop calling me, I don't give magic lessons!" That evening, before going to bed, I called Gustavo Lorgia again and explained what magic meant to me and why I wanted to learn his craft, to which he responded: "I expect you at my home on Saturday at 8AM."

My efforts rewarded me with the privilege of learning from the greatest Colombian magician of his time and, thanks to him, I also learned from other national greats like Richard Sarmiento and Jose Simhon. But, if this wasn't enough, Tamariz, Carrol and Ballesteros – the same ones who amazed me that night in that small theater – also became my teachers who taught me great things at that moment in my life. Perhaps, the most important lesson I learned from the experience is the one that my friend Juan Pablo Neira, who shares my love of magic, stated when he said, "life is an illusion, a product of our imagination."

These two experiences defined some crucial elements of my essence and personality that, until today, has determined the road I have taken.

You have to jump into the void to chase dreams, even though they are often hard to realize. I had the good fortune of having these experiences while I was still a child, and, as I mentioned, they had a great influence on me. Today, from the perspective of a father of four, I see with concern how our children and young people are being educated – both at home and in schools – with a vision focused on overprotection, which doesn't allow them to discover the importance of risk taking. This is something we need to learn early in life. From our childhood, we should discover the exhilaration of being able to dream, knowing that obstacles and challenges will appear along the way. It teaches us that stumbling and falling are a part of life. We must understand that what we call "failure" is a key part of the growth process, through which we learn to recover from adversity and overcome the trials that we face in life, where we need to stand up and keep fighting. Perseverance is often the only way to learn.

We need to prepare our children to avoid falling into the slumber that keeps us from overcoming adversity. This slumber is like a collective state of being in "autopilot," replete with repetitive routines in the home, at work, or with our social lives. We know we have an infinite capacity to grow, to create, to transform; however, we often don't know how to fully utilize this capacity and it often stymies our ability to realize our dreams. We can't allow that slumber to extinguish our entrepreneurial flame.

We need children and young people who can dream, who are courageous, and who can understand the importance of knowing and learning from failure. As the saying goes, "What is important is not to avoid failure, but to learn from failure." As workers, we need brave souls to propose unorthodox methods, break paradigms, and present challenging and disruptive ideas that can, more often than not, accelerate progress in ways we never envisioned. Our society also needs resilient families and politicians willing to tackle big projects with integrity that consistently serve the common good. It is vitally important to grasp that we all have enormous potential and the only way we can leave our footprint in the world is to unlock that potential in our lives.

Is it possible that we are already making the best use of our capabilities? Do we have the desire to undertake projects to leave a better world for our children and future generations?

It is important to realize that there is a giant sleeping within each of us. If we are able to awaken that giant then miracles can happen. That giant, and those miracles, are a manifestation of realized potential that symbolize the power of entrepreneurship. Throughout this book, I intend to try and to awaken your sleeping giant in the hope that by doing so, I can strive to be a coauthor of your dreams.

The pages that follow are divided into three sections: the first section, contained in chapters I and II, present a general context of entrepreneurship; the second section, chapter III, relate my personal experience, which has provided the foundation for the Attitude E Framework, and illustrates that entrepreneurship is a bit of a roller-coaster and finally the third block, chapters IV to X, present an in-depth look at the Attitude E Framework.

I hope you will enjoy reading these pages as much as I enjoyed writing them. It is my earnest hope that they will help you discover and realize the potential of your entrepreneurial spirit and capability.

Again, thank you for your trust!

CHAPTER I

THE POWER TO VENTURE

*Twenty years from now you will be more disappointed by
the things you didn't do than by the ones you did do.*

MARK TWAIN

Although this is not a book about the etymology or history of
entrepreneurship, it is important to put into context its origins
and evolution, so we can understand how thinkers, academia
and the media have influenced how we presently understand
and apply the concept.

The term entrepreneur was first used by an Irish economist
of French descent, Richard Cantillon (1697-1734), who chal-
lenged the classic and neoclassical economists who theorized
that markets were characterized by a state of perfect knowledge
and certainty by writing Essai Sur la Nature the Commerce en
General, published posthumously in 1755. In this book, Cantillon theorized that the market is full of uncertainty and it is required to face dilemmas, take risks, and invest in order to expect
an economic return. Therefore, those best qualified to perform
this function are business people, otherwise known as entrepreneurs. His great contribution was to introduce and associate en-

trepreneurship with the concept of uncertainty, a link studied in depth by 20th century economists Ludwig von Mises, Frank Knight, and John M. Keynes, who then developed their own academic theories about uncertainty.

Cantillon was followed by the French economist and industrial entrepreneur Jean-Baptiste Say (1767-1832), who contributed to the use of the term entrepreneur after studying the works of Adam Smith, whom he greatly admired. Say found that the Scottish philosopher and economist did not take into account the role of the entrepreneur. He thus borrowed the concept from Cantillon and built his theses upon it; among them, he states that the entrepreneur is an economic agent who generates a product or service by using resources such as land, capital, and labor, and that he is the one who has the capability of re-appropriating inefficiently-used resources in a productive manner.

The Austrian economist and politician Joseph Schumpeter (1883-1950), considered one of the great economists of the 20th century, made important contributions to the study and development of the theories of entrepreneurship. In 1932, after a career that included finance minister of Austria, he moved to Boston to become a professor at Harvard. It was there he perfected his theories of entrepreneurship, known as Mark I and Mark II.

In Mark I, Schumpeter argued that the innovations and technological developments of nations were the product of entrepreneurs, or "wild spirits," as he also called them. He declared that innovation is the critical component of economic change, and he argued that innovation-based markets produce better results than the invisible hand and price competition espoused by classical theory. This contribution is foundational, because when he associated innovation with entrepreneurship, he opened a tantalizing door, full of possibilities. He proposed the concept of creative destruction, and he introduced a German term, unternehmergeist, which means 'entrepreneurial spirit.' He also proposed that "doing new things or doing things already being done, but in a different way" is the direct result of the efforts of entrepreneurs.

In Mark II, he contributes the theory that it is large companies that foster innovation and economic growth, because they have the necessary scale, capital and resources to invest in research and development, which allows them to create better products and services at lower prices for consumers. Specifically, Schumpeter hinted, even within large companies, that it is necessary to incentivize unternehmergeist, which equips employees to become agents of creative destruction to accelerate innovation and development.

Until this point, studies and theories illustrating how entrepreneurs were essential for economic development had come from economists. However, American psychologist David McClelland (1917-1998) made his contributions from a psychological perspective, identifying the attributes of the entrepreneur in his studies on motivation, needs, and achievement. McClelland stated that all human beings could be classified according to three types of motivational needs: achievement, authority/power, and affiliation. He concluded that entrepreneurs are individuals motivated by achievement, and that they are characterized by their capacity to assume risk.

Peter Drucker, known as the father of management, made

his contributions to the theory of entrepreneurship in 1964 when he asserted that the entrepreneur is the individual who seeks change, responds to it, and takes advantage of opportunities. He later stated in 1985 that entrepreneurship is neither a science nor an art, but a practice that is not limited to the private sector.

These are some of the most important historical contributions in the evolution of the study and science of entrepreneurship. There are many other people from myriad disciplines who have contributed, in one way or another; furthermore, there is an ample supply of literature on the subject. My goal is to provide a general overview without going into an in-depth study on the history and evolution of the concept of entrepreneurship. I endeavor, rather, to share a brief and general journey to put into context and explain, from a high-level perspective, where the term comes from.

Today, thanks to the Internet and social media, many more people are capable of publishing their theories and thoughts. An interesting and valuable example is Entrepreneurship Is, created by Babson College, where anyone can participate and share their definitions of entrepreneurship. Every definition found within this portal is magnificent and full of meaning. I have randomly chosen some to illustrate how the concept is currently perceived and interpreted:

"If you have intellect, imagination and passion to identify and meet needs, you are an entrepreneur. Entrepreneurship invites all those who have the drive and vision to recognize and

create opportunities."

"It is recognizing an opportunity to change the world with a great idea."

"It is the skill to overcome obstacles and barriers using imagination and innovation."

"Entrepreneurship is passion, resourcefulness, and drive."

"Ambition and spirit, combined in a set of skills that allow you to create your own journey."

"An entrepreneur is a humble person who is always able to get the best from others."

"Entrepreneurship is identifying an opportunity. Assuming risks. Committing to succeed."

"It is risking everything."

"It is thinking outside the box."

It is worth it to visit the site and review the contributions, which are now more than three thousand. You are also welcome to contribute your own!

Beyond the evolution of the concept of entrepreneurship, it is valuable and important to understand how and when it began to be included as an area of study in colleges and universities. Entrepreneurship first appears as a subject of study in 1947 in an academic program at Harvard University. However, it was not until the end of the 1970s that the term started to appear in the catalogs of pre-graduate and graduate programs. Jeff Timmons, from Babson College, forecasted in the early 1980s that education in entrepreneurship would be the new wave of transformation in business education. It is significant that Babson College has since been setting the bar for this field of study throughout the world, and is now recognized as the cradle of entrepreneurship education.

Most business schools worldwide now have entrepreneurship-related content that is also offered as electives for students in other fields. In certain countries, some schools have even started including in their curriculum subjects that prepare students to take risks, structure their ideas, and plan businesses. This initiative is welcomed because an early age is ideal to start encouraging and promoting entrepreneurship, and will undoubtedly result in preparing youth to face a world full of challenges while equipping them with the tools to become better individuals and better professionals.

We can see that, from its origins, the concept of entrepreneurship has been associated with the capacity to dream, and the ability to then convert those dreams into reality. Although its pioneers came from the economic and industrial world, with time, people have started using the term in other contexts. It is currently used mainly in the field of enterprise creation. Governments seek to establish policies and legislation to promote entrepreneurship, and academic institutions conduct rigorous studies defining the attributes and characteristics of successful entrepreneurs. There are platforms and contests that exist to create and fund business plans, as well as investment ecosystems, venture capital funds, and incubators that have been created to support and encourage start-ups. There have even been reality shows on television focused on the process of the business entrepreneur.

All of these efforts are valid and necessary, but it is important to reach beyond. It is evident that the business creator is an entrepreneur, and that entrepreneurship, seen from this perspective, is essential for economic development. However, constraining ourselves to this narrow view diminishes the full potential of the concept of entrepreneurship, because it is limited to those who create businesses. And although the person who creates a business is an entrepreneur, not all entrepreneurs create businesses. We need to find ways to develop, activate, and leverage the entrepreneurial potential that we all have inside, and imbue an entrepreneurial attitude in our educational systems, governments, organizations, and workforces, in order to foster progress alongside our individual and collective development.

It's in this spirit that Babson College has launched, among its many contributions to the field, the Entrepreneurship of All Kinds initiative, meant to promote the entrepreneurial spirit and develop entrepreneurial capabilities throughout the disciplines. In its opening page, Babson describes the initiative as follows:

> *Our rapidly changing world demands entrepreneurship of all kinds. Today we need entrepreneurs at all levels in all types of organizations to create opportunities, implement solutions and collaborate with others to turn visions into reality.*

Entrepreneurship, and the reinforcement of an entrepreneurial attitude, is what will generate transformation and progress in individuals, institutions, and nations.

This is the motivation that drives me to write this book, and to also promote this idea through keynote speeches and various other methods. My intention is to awaken the power of individual and collective entrepreneurship to enable us to positively transform our present world, and to leave our children and later generations a better future with greater opportunities.

Entrepreneurship has transformational power; however, we must not forget that this activity is always accompanied by high levels of uncertainty, and is therefore subject to fear. Let's try to recall some time in our lives when we tried to start something. It could be anything, but it's important to visualize and reconstruct what we felt the moment we made the decision to pursue this dream or work on that project. Very likely, our initial feeling was one of excitement, although possibly accompanied by uncertainty as questions popped up, and we may have then been invaded by fear after not being able to immediately find all the answers. This is natural, but these feelings sometimes stop us from taking risks or starting new projects; we are afraid of jumping into the void and taking the risk to transform our ideas, our projects, and our dreams into realities.

We need to strengthen our ability to face uncertainty and overcome that fear. It's worth it! According to the following metaphor presented by Nick Udall, CEO of nowhere, entrepreneurs are those people who learn to dance with the known and unknown to make sense of the world and "transform the unknown into known, the unconscious into conscious, and the invisible into visible."

We have the capability of starting projects that are strictly personal: learning a new language, learning to play a musical instrument, start or complement our education, gain or lose weight, run a marathon, or climb a mountain. These personal endeavors make us grow, improve, and transform ourselves, all so we can be of service to others.

If you work in an organization – whether in government, business, or nonprofit – you also have the power to initiate and assume an entrepreneurial attitude to grow and develop your career. LinkedIn co-founder Eric Hoffman and Ben Casnocha state in their book, The Startup of YOU, that the competition for job opportunities is increasingly fierce, and the old model of job stability is a thing of the past. They propose that the key to manage our professional careers and accelerate them in this competitive market is to view them as a startup. Why? Because both startups and the entrepreneurs who manage them are agile, invest in themselves, build networks, take risks, and use uncertainty and volatility in their favor. These – the authors emphasize – are the same skills professionals need to develop to advance their careers.

In turn, when we assume an entrepreneurial attitude at work, we are contributing more to the organization where we work than we would at a routine job. I was recently in a meeting with the Vice-President of Human Resources of a large organization; he had a big office with a stunning view of the city, from which he could also see the company floor, full of people working away. We were discussing the power of entrepreneurial attitude when I saw how his gaze suddenly seemed lost when he looked at his team working across the glass. After a few seconds of silence, in a reflective voice, he asked me, "Can you imagine what would happen if all of these people, who are here performing their routine jobs, were able to contribute all their ideas to co-create the growth and development of this company?"

We have so much to offer, but we keep it bottled inside! Why? On one hand, this happens because of our fear in the face of uncertainty; on the other hand, because organizations themselves are diminishing the entrepreneurial capacity that we still have. Only organizations that have models for fostering and managing innovation and internal entrepreneurship are progressing, growing, and generating more value.

The family can and should be viewed as an enterprise. The decision to get married is a clear example, as is having children, educating them, and supporting them as they grow. But the reality is we don't realize it. A relative told me that we are so absorbed by our work that we don't focus our highest attention on the most transcendental of our endeavors and the most meaningful job we have: the family, which as the nucleus of society needs to be healthy, grow, and evolve. We slip into mechanical routines that remove excitement and potential from family life, and we see more marriages end, more children lost, and more people succumb to the temptation of their vices as a result. We haven't yet been able to quantify the effect this has on people's productivity and on the development of our societies. This is why we need to view the family as an ongoing endeavor and passionately fulfill our lives as couples, as well as our roles as parents and children.

We live in a world filled with deprivation. We need only open one eye to discover injustice, inequality, and unmet needs. Faced with this, we can assume a passive and indifferent attitude, or we can be willing to contribute by assuming an entrepreneurial attitude. We probably all feel a sense of powerlessness in the face of so much deprivation, and we ask ourselves: "Where can I begin? What can I do to make a difference?" When Craig Kielburger, founder and director of Free the Children, asked Mother Teresa of Calcutta these frustrated questions, she wisely responded, "When you try to help others, you will never be able to do great things. You will just be able to do small things, but with great love."

It is through one action, one act of faith, taking one step after another, that you can gain the possibility to revolutionize generosity and redefine happiness. Nothing can make us happier than helping others without expecting anything in return. If we close our eyes and try to relive the happiest moments we have had – not counting those that are obvious, like the birth of our children – surely they will be moments when we have shared with authentic generosity or we have helped someone in need.

A friend who lives in Miami sent me an e-mail in early 2008, in which he attached a photo of an overflowing river. The image was impactful. In his message, he explained that it was the Mira River, in Tumaco, Colombia, and told me about the magnitude of the flooding that had left more than seven thousand families homeless. He also asked me if I could help in any way after suggesting I contact Beatriz Corredor, a woman who was assisting in the area. He sent the message to all his friends to ask for their solidarity in making a call to action to face this tragedy. My first thought was, "What can I do about something so big and far away?" Several weeks passed, and I did nothing until the day I listened to Craig Kielburger quote that sentence from Mother Teresa during a keynote in Bogota. I then recalled the picture of the river, and I decided to write to Beatriz. I said I was ready to help and awaited a response. I thought she would ask for some material things I could buy and somehow send to Tumaco. However, I was overwhelmed when I read her response. She simply asked me to contact an organization in England called Shelterbox that provides help by sending boxes that contain everything a family needs to live for up to two years when they have lost everything in a disaster. Each box contains a tent, blankets, a cooktop, pots and pans, dishes, flashlights, a water purification kit, a tool box, and toys. I decided to write to them to let them know what had happened, and attached the photo. I received their response the next day. It was not very encouraging, because they said that they would unfortunately be unable to travel to Colombia for security reasons. But something inside me demanded, "Insist!" I wrote back to them, almost begging them to please reconsider.

To my surprise, they responded a couple of days later saying they would come. A group of people arrived in Tumaco sometime later to diagnose the situation. It was very exciting when they generously donated 100 boxes for the victims of the floods. The boxes arrived and were given to the families that were sleeping on the floors of the local school.

It was an undoubtedly gratifying experience, because although I felt I had done very little, the impact on the victims was very significant. Of course this made me really happy. And I thought the story had ended there, but I had no idea it was just starting!

Three years later, Colombia was hit by massive flooding after the worst rainy season in the country's history. It wasn't seven thousand families without homes this time, but four million people. I remembered the experience in Tumaco, and using the relationship that had been established with the management at Shelterbox, I decided to send them another email. They responded promptly, and in an exchange of messages we recalled the experience we had shared in Colombia three years back. They then sent several teams to verify, with their own eyes, the magnitude of the disaster. They didn't send a hundred boxes this time – they sent six thousand! It was a gesture of solidarity that touched me deeply. It was wonderful to witness the tents being erected in different areas of the country and participate in an experience in which people, businesses and governmental institutions joined efforts to contribute to the success of the mission. But what was more impactful was seeing the glimpses of hope in the eyes of the people and families affected by the tragedy as they saw the tents going up. Although a temporary solution, the tents gave them reasons to feel energized, encouraged, and hopeful.

I present these examples because I believe they illustrate how entrepreneurship can transform us as people, families, professionals, and agents of social change.

As people, it changes us by turning us into permanently curious individuals, allowing us to discover the importance of knowing we can always be better, and that it is very gratifying to improve ourselves. It also transforms our families, because these experiences help us to avoid becoming stuck in routine and monotony, while also injecting excitement into marriage and the process of raising our children. In our business and work life, because it makes us feel the drive – every day – to be not just people who perform defined duties, but people who generate, articulate, communicate, and execute ideas. Finally, I am convinced that this journey helps society progress, and the world can indeed become a better place if we jumpstart our potential to contribute, help, and work to fulfill the urgent needs that are right in front of us.

Recently, after delivering a keynote speech to a team at a government institution in Colombia, I received a message from one of the participants, from which I share the following extract:

> *Felipe, thank you for awakening me from my slumber. As the years go by, I feel I have lost my drive and want to risk less. Perhaps I have worked tirelessly all my life and I don't want to lose what I have obtained with much effort. Today I discovered that I can jump into the void, and that I just need to dream and believe in that dream!*

These words, so sincere, reflect the feelings and reality of many people throughout the world, no matter their age, location, profession, or activity. And I ask myself: Do we identify with this woman's message? Do we also feel submerged in the slumber she mentions? Are we full of dreams we haven't realized? Do we know about this immense potential that we have, now lying dormant?

Well, the time has come to awaken all our capabilities! To live life in all its dimensions, employing the entrepreneurial attitude I have repeatedly detailed. Only then will we be able to maximize the potential we have to make our dreams possible and become true creative agents. We are unique human beings possessing qualities and talents, who with passion and service, can do our share to positively transform the world.

CHAPTER II

THE ENTREPRENEURIAL ATTITUDE

There Are Three Types of People: Those Who Make Things
Happen, Those Who Watch Things Happen, and
Those Who Wonder What Happened

NICHOLAS MURRAY BUTLER

Without a doubt, the most important part of this journey in learning about the art of entrepreneurship has been the reflection on my own life and experiences. From these moments, I have been able to extract some ideas that, later on and with time, have been enriching. I found kindred spirits in the biographies of great entrepreneurs from different disciplines, and as I talk with individuals who have made entrepreneurship a lifestyle, I learned that there are leaders who have been able to create an entrepreneurial culture within their respective organizations.

We can always find people who have truly excelled no matter what their life choices have been. In the world of music, we had Ludwig Van Beethoven and John Lennon: the former, an icon of classical music, and the latter, a rock luminary. They both made their marks in the history of music. In sports, we find soccer players like Pelé or Lionel Messi, cyclists like Lucho Herrera or Nairo Quintana, athletes like Catherine Ibarguen or Gabrielle Douglas, who demonstrate how having passion for their arts as well as discipline have led them to excellence. In the political sphere, we have Winston Churchill and Nelson Mandela who inspired millions of people with their messages and served as role models by leading from example for many world leaders. In the spiritual world, we find people like Mother Teresa and Pope Francis, who have left, and continue to leave, a notable mark on our spiritual legacy.

But the truth is that you don't need to be a celebrity or historical figure to excel. We often find exceptional individuals in our everyday lives that make a difference and stand out from the crowd. There are examples of children who shine in their academic pursuits, others with athletic ability or musical talents. There are mothers or fathers that exercise self-sacrifice in the wellbeing of their families, others that provide for their households, and others still that display integrity and mastery in matters of faith, pedagogy, medicine, and a host of other topics and professions whose actions are all worthy of admiration.

We see something similar in the business world. We can find pioneers and paragons in private, government, academic, and non-profit institutions. From salespeople who systematically break their own records and find ways of selling more to leaders who have a special ability to connect with their teams. These leaders are capable of motivating and aligning teams to achieve extraordinary results. But, again, salespeople and leaders are not the only ones in business that have demonstrated a commitment to excellence in their fields, there are also accountants, engineers, lawyers, secretaries, and many others that are constantly improving themselves.

After studying all of these cases I found many common-alities in certain behaviors and characteristics that permit us to learn a lot on how to best employ the entrepreneurial attitude.

The behaviors and characteristics of these individuals are as follows:

- They have a special talent.
- They have a clear vision of what they want to accom-plish.
- They always have a clear action plan on how to best achieve their goals and they review this plan on a regu-lar basis.
- They face adversity with determination and view fail-ure as an opportunity to learn.
- They are persistent even in the face of failure.
- They surround themselves with like-minded individu-als and understand the intrinsic value of teamwork.
- They are always defying the status quo to discover solu-tions to problems or obstacles that frequently arise.
- They challenge themselves daily to find ways of doing better today what they did very well yesterday.
- They have a higher purpose in life and are often fo-cused on serving others.
- They are alert to new opportunities and to make the most of each and every situation.

But if I had to summarize in a single sentence what all of these people have in common, it is that every one of them, without exception, live their lives convinced that:

- Any situation, no matter how great, can be improved.

41

This, in essence, is an attitude.

Attitude is how we choose our position toward life. It determines our bias toward a person, place, object, or event. The attitude we assume is always determined by our past but is defined by our present. It is a response to conscious or unconscious factors in our mind. In contrast to our personality, which tends to be unique and fixed, our attitude can change and adapt in response to our circumstances. If we so choose, we can have a negative attitude toward some situations in our lives while having a positive attitude toward others. We can also have a passive attitude toward certain personal or professional challenges, but it is important—essential even—to have a truly active response to the challenges we face.

John C. Maxwell stated that attitude has a profound impact on our lives. No matter what we do, it is our attitude that will determine the dynamics of our relationships. It is the way we react to failure and obstacles that define our perception of success. Attitude can make or break us.

This seemingly revelatory but common sense truth that attitude determines one's behavior allows us to conceive of powerful scenarios in professional and personal spheres. It all depends on how we use this understanding. Our behavior depends on the attitude we adopt with respect to a person or situation. Therefore, our attitude has the power to influence those around us and, in turn, their attitudes can modify our own. We cannot take this simple truth for granted because, in actuality, all of our actions will determine how we communicate and relate with others as well as establish mutual understanding. Our attitude will determine how we approach our work as well as relate to our subordinates, peers, and superiors. In addition, we cannot forget the importance that our attitudes have in building the most important relationships that we have: our family.

Although I have been asserting that having talent or aptitude in a given field is essential, we cannot rely on ability alone to reach our definition of success. After all, there are many talented people who are stuck in their careers and are still searching for meaning in their lives. Our skills or abilities, while essential, are insufficient to meeting the above criteria; there has to be something more.

Looking around we can find many others who, in spite of knowing they are excellent in their field of expertise, possess a strong aptitude, or variety of different talents are stubbornly still focused on their egos and believe that this is enough to conquer the world. In so doing, they step on those who stand in their way, humiliate others, and feed their selfishness while they search for success without considering the consequences. It is their attitude that often leaves them with problems and obstacles that, in many cases, will lead them in the opposite direction of what they seek. By adopting such an attitude, they set themselves up for failure.

To delve a bit deeper into this topic, I want to highlight someone whom I consider to be one of the great thought leaders of business excellence. It is someone who has had a tremendous influence on my life and career: Jim Collins. Jim is an author, professor, consultant, and expert in the areas of excellence and organizational sustainability. In his book, Good to Great, he studies companies that have managed to evolve from being good to becoming extraordinary. He found that great companies share several similarities between them, and I want to touch upon the first of these conditions.

According to his analysis, companies that have become extraordinary have been led by individuals, he calls, "level 5 leaders." He describes them as leaders that possess a synthesis of different leadership styles that strongly contribute to the success of their organizations. These leaders are often incredibly talented individuals but are still capable of approaching situations with humility while still having the fierce resolve necessary to achieving their goals.

Great talent is the result from possessing an aptitude and combining it with discipline, perseverance, and interest. Humility, on the other hand, defines an attitude that determines how we influence others and allow ourselves to be influenced by them. Lastly, fierce resolve focuses our efforts towards achieving results while providing for consistent extraordinary execution. This model for success derives from the philosophical theory that all human beings have three capabilities: reason, will, and affect. Finding a balance among them and developing them equitably will make us better people.

Zig Ziglar, veteran of the Second World War, said: "Your attitude, not your aptitude, will determine your altitude." This sentence, besides being inspiring, is quite accurate. Although talent is important, a great talent with the wrong attitude is the perfect formula for failure. A great attitude, acting individually, is no guarantee of success. Therefore, it is important to find a way to work on both aspects so we can achieve 'altitude' in our lives.

One of the most notorious characteristics of attitude is its ability to enact positive elements within different life sectors.

When we surround ourselves with people that have positive, optimistic and constructive attitudes, it is much more probable that we too, can not only experience similar sentiments but develop them ourselves. By adopting such attitudes, we become agents that can then transmit these positive elements to others. Now, let me ask you a question: Is there anything more contagious than a positive attitude? The answer is yes: a negative attitude! If, in a group of fifty people, there is one with a negative, pessimistic or destructive attitude, it is almost certain that it will spread to the group. This type of individual poses an enormous risk in not only our own personal development but that on a professional scale as well.

People ask me often: Who can live with a good attitude all the time and in all aspects of life? To this I say that we live in a complex and competitive world filled with problems everywhere, and it's not easy to adopt a positive attitude all the time. This is reality. We are exposed to the positive and negative influences of our environment and to the fact that our attitude adapts to the context of where we are. One could also ask, how much control do we have over our attitude? Can we mold it so that it plays in our favor? Is it possible to help someone with a negative attitude and potentially convert it into a positive one? Of course! While it is easier to maintain a current worldview—that can often be destructive— it can be modified. It is not permanent. There is an ample amount of literature dealing with this subject, some of which I have mentioned in the previous pages.

I would like to make it clear that a change in attitude can make all the difference, no matter how complicated the situation or how complex the decision, a change in our attitude can allow us to see the situation with a different lens. This is why we need to become an engineer of our attitude, one that can properly analyze and design a way forward that can determine our reactions to the consequences of much of our lives. Similarly, we need to be alert to those around us, especially those we can influence. By helping others to change their attitudes, we become active agents in the transformation of people around us. These contributions to others will always return their weight in gold. As I previously mentioned, surrounding ourselves with others that practice a positive attitude can have as much of an impact on our ability to maintain one as we can ourselves.

You can probably guess where I am heading. I would like to invite you all to assume an entrepreneurial attitude in our lives that allows us to see in ourselves the possibility of becoming better: better individuals, better parents and spouses, better children, better professionals, better employees or better managers.

I believe that the best form of personal growth is imagining ourselves as individuals full of potential. We have the ability to evolve, to learn, and to live new experiences. We need to see deficiencies or issues as spaces full of opportunities to love and grow. This allows us to see our work places as vehicles to generate new ideas. By adopting this viewpoint, we can perform our jobs with commitment and efficiency, which ultimately permits us to contribute more to the success of our organizations and subsequently to the development and satisfaction of our customers and partners. But this view extends beyond the workplace and the home. By adopting this attitude, it can expand our worldview beyond the local or regional, it can allow us to even see our country as a universe filled with opportunities to contribute to and help in its continual and lasting development.

By opening our eyes, by observing within and around us, we realize that we live in a world of possibilities. In unlocking these possibilities, the hallmark of the entrepreneurial spirit, we can not only enjoy life, but we can become agents of change to make the most of the potential we have in any situation.

The Attitude E framework is an attempt to supply you with an easy methodology to unleash the power within yourself. It is intended to be easy to follow and to generate extraordinary results at multiple levels: personal, professional, familial, etc. The reason for this is that a change in attitude can ripple across all aspects of our lives.

The Attitude E approach is made up of six attributes that if practiced and applied, will provide you with an entrepreneurial attitude where the opportunities of which I spoke, and the earnestness of seeing possibilities where there were once obstacles, is made manifest.

These attributes, all denoted by the letter 'E', serve as the foundation for embracing an entrepreneurial attitude: Envisioning, Energy, Endurance, Ensemble, Elasticity, and Engagement. But before we delve deeper into the framework itself and each of its elements, I would first like to tell you the stories that inspired it.

CHAPTER III

THE ROLLER COASTER

"The journey is the reward."

I would now like to unpretentiously share some of the factual parts of my professional journey. I've decided to do this because there've been many who've taught me valuable lessons I want to include in this book. I know there are thousands of stories more powerful and inspiring than mine, so I don't intend for this chapter to be autobiographical, or a narcissistic paean to my own story. This book is not about me! On the contrary: it's about you, the reader, and it's mostly devoted to describing the experiences of many other people who have traveled roads as they have pursued their dreams. Through these stories, I hope that you will discover your own immense capacity to create and to transform – or to even start a new venture – and that they will serve as a basis to illustrate the ideas and concepts presented throughout this book.

Let me start with my own journey. In 1995, I graduated with a bachelor's degree in business administration from the

University of the Andes in Bogota. At a time when interactive technologies like the Internet were becoming en vogue, I decided – with my great friend and partner in madness, Juan Fernando Santos – to start a company dedicated to leveraging them by using computers to develop interactive media, an innovation that became fashionable with the launch of Mosaic, the first graphical internet browser. We started Ink with a workspace generously provided to us by Juan Fernando's father, Reynaldo, whose office was located on 94th street in Bogota.

We received a call one day from Harry Child, an interesting visionary who, in association with Corferias, annually organized the specialized trade show Expo-Construction and Expo-Design. Mr. Child was interested in promoting that year's event using CD-ROMs and a website. Looking back, I am not sure whether it was talent or drive he recognized in us. Whatever it was, he hired us to develop his digital promotional pieces, which turned out great and ended up contributing to the success of the tradeshow. This successful project led to a new project, and that one to another. We suddenly had enough work to require our own office and employees. I still recall the emotion I felt when we purchased new computers from MacPoint, a company that would later on become one of our clients.

Another partnership began when Vladdo, the well-known journalist and cartoonist who used to write the weekly technology column at Semana, the leading magazine publisher in Colombia, ended up by coincidence in our offices one day, resulting in the start of a wonderful friendship. This visit also resulted in Semana Publications becoming one of our customers. When Vladdo later on made plans to travel abroad for a year, he asked if Juan Fernando and I could write the technology review column in his absence, an offer we accepted. We devoted ourselves to writing articles for the readers of Semana, discussing subjects such as the advances in digital convergence, the benefits of interactivity, and the promise of the Internet. We obtained wide public exposure through this publishing venture, which allowed us to provide advise to several companies about these topics, gradually enabling us to become pioneers and evangelizers of the digital economy in Colombia. Each experience led us to meet more people. It was a chain reaction that allowed us to attract new clients and grow our business.

It so happened that Nicolas Dueñas, a former classmate, great friend, and all-around brilliant and passionate Ecuadorian, visited us one day to give his farewells before returning to his home country. During our conversation, when he learned about how much we had grown, and details about what we offered, he excitedly proposed a series of visits and presentations in Ecuador. We arrived there not long after, traveling back and forth while generating interest in the people we met with, and acquiring new Ecuadorian clients. Nicolas became our business partner, who now shared our dream.

As you have probably recognized, the first years of our company were successful. We were excited to experience the growth of Ink while also taking great care to protect the reputation we were creating along the way. We felt proud satisfaction upon seeing the fruits of our efforts, and we were also creating jobs and contributing to the development of a new industry in our country.

Despite what we had achieved, problems beset us in 1998,

when a deep economic crisis hit our country. This had a dramatic impact on our company, which by now had 25 employees in Colombia and Ecuador. Sales started to fall, accounts receivable were not paid, and our cash flow was far from what we had projected. To make matters worse, if it was raining in Colombia, it was pouring in Ecuador. The economic instability that hit Ecuador was a big blow for us. Our main customer in Ecuador was the Banco Popular del Ecuador (National People's Bank) for whom we had built, among other things, an Internet banking platform that had been the first virtual banking service in the country. We were caught off-guard by a government intervention to the bank, claimed to be in response to unexplained scandals. All ongoing projects were cancelled, and all our bank accounts, which happened to be in that same institution, were disastrously frozen. We were denied access to the funds we had accumulated during our years of work in Ecuador; funds that were supposed to be our buffer to face the crisis we found ourselves in.

Defying the situation, in August 1998 I married Pilar, the woman who has been my motivation and my unconditional partner. When we returned from our honeymoon, we found that the owner of the offices we were renting had garnished the company's bank accounts. We owed back rent, and although we assured him we would pay, our word was not enough. In addition to this debt, we owed back pay to our employees, as we didn't have the funds to pay them. We were also behind in payroll and other taxes. It was a time of stress, confusion, and frustration. We couldn't understand how an excellent idea could be ruined by external factors that were not related to the business itself, nor our ability to make the most of our business opportunities.

Life, however, was generous to us, and we soon received a stroke of luck. In 1998 and 1999, the same years when the economy in our countries was so depressed and hard-hit, the world saw a tremendous rise in interest in Internet-related businesses. We saw other entrepreneurs who were able to obtain millions of dollars to start their projects with nothing more than a business plan. Those with available capital were almost desperately looking for investment opportunities due to the potential for large, rapid returns.

That is how we were able to use our previous accomplishments, and a new business plan, to convince three important Colombian business groups to invest ten million dollars to expand our business throughout Latin America despite the dark economic climate, with the goal of becoming the premier interactive media agency in the region. In retrospect, I feel stunned by how fine the line is between scarcity and abundance, between despair and hope, between failure and success, and between sadness and joy.

Our company had entered a new stage due to these developments; we had a clear mandate, and we had to execute it. We acquired a company in Chile, and opened new offices in Buenos Aires, Sao Paulo, San Jose (Costa Rica), Mexico City, and Miami. We understood that we needed to hire the best talent, and we tried our best to do so. Many of our employees were hired out of Harvard and Stanford. An additional part of our strategy was to have offices in the best parts of town, which is why we established them on Lincoln Road in Miami, Parque de la 93 in Bogota, Las Condes in Santiago, and Polanco in Mexico City. In nine months, we had managed to conceive and give birth to a regional company with a presence in eight countries, and with a staff of three hundred to make the most of our massive potential. We moved to Costa Rica in 1999, and I was assigned the responsibility of managing our market in Central America and the Caribbean.

We started selling and implementing projects all over the continent while excitedly observing how similar companies in the United States and Europe were growing very rapidly, with valuations reaching unbelievable levels. I remember feeling great when benchmark companies in our industry like Scient, Sapient or Zefer were being valued at thirty times sales; that is, if a company had annual sales of one million dollars, it was valued at thirty million dollars. The math was simple: in one quarter we had sold $1.5 million in consulting and development projects, which annualized to $6 million per year. Multiplying this figure by thirty, we arrived at the attractive valuation of one hundred and eighty million dollars. Both Intel Capital and Sapient, another large American company, were interested in our company, and we explored investment and acquisition opportunities with them. Whether we retained one, three, or ten percent of the company, we would be millionaires! But I wish we had known what was coming.

Our fifteen minutes of fame lasted three years. In April 2001, what we now recognize as the dot-com bubble completely burst. Our company predictably did not escape this terrible maelstrom. Our valuation plummeted, and the interest from Intel Capital and Sapient disappeared. Our dreams of early retirement went up in smoke. We had no choice but to close our offices in Costa Rica and Mexico, which I was responsible for carrying out. After

I finished this difficult task, I was notified there was no longer a role for me at my own company, and I lost my job.

This happened a few weeks after Juan Martin, our first son, was born. And right after we had decided that my wife would stop working to devote her time to the baby! As a couple, we had transitioned from DINKs (Dual Income, No Kids) to NIOKs (No Income, One Kid). Just as before, I had experienced the fine line between failure and success.

However, my wife kept her cool. Gifting me with her wisdom, she recommended that I consider using this time to continue my education and earn a master's degree, an idea I had previously tossed around, but not pursued. I decided to follow her advice, and I ended up being accepted to start my postgraduate studies at IMD in Lausanne, a spectacular city in French Switzerland. We arrived on January 2, 2002, and spent an unforgettable year there.

We were delighted daily by the imposing view of the snow-covered Swiss Alps and the deep blue of Lake Geneva. It was both a wonderful academic experience and an incredible life opportunity. We built beautiful friendships, discovered the magic of the seasons, used the opportunity to take weekend getaways to other countries, and came to understand that the apparent rigidity of the Swiss included a profound respect toward harmony and family. These were some of the reasons we considered searching for opportunities to stay in Europe. Naturally, it was not easy for a Colombian family, lacking resident visas, and during a depressed labor market. But we decided to try. Toward the end of the program, there were two job opportunities that looked very promising.

However, something happened on graduation day that changed our plans. The university invited an alumnus of the class of 1978 to speak at the ceremony. As the epitome of a successful businessman, he was asked to share his experiences and give advice to those of us who were about to graduate and head back to the real world to create a better future for ourselves. His name was Woods Staton, and while he possessed a "gringo" name and appearance, he was also a native Colombian who boasted the sagacity and cunning of the enterprising paisas of his hometown of Medellin. I still vividly remember the thunderous applause he received at the podium from all the graduates, relatives, professors, and staff at the end of his memorable speech. By an unlikely coincidence, my classmates had chosen me to deliver a speech on behalf of the graduating class during the ceremony. This is how two Colombians ended up delivering speeches in a room with representatives from over fifty countries. This quirk of fate also allowed me to meet Woods, a great man who would teach me so much, and with whom I would forge a lasting friendship.

After the speeches and applause had ended, Woods and I started talking, and we engaged in a lively dialogue at the graduation party hosted in the grand ballroom of the iconic Bon Rivage Hotel. I passionately shared my dreams with him while he listened attentively and also shared fascinating stories of his life. We talked about our speeches, our families, and our children, who happened to be the same age. We also discussed the possibility of expanding Endeavor to Colombia. Their mission was to foster entrepreneurship, and Woods held a seat on the board of directors.

As the evening progressed, one idea led to another, and one project to another, until he suddenly and unexpectedly proposed we work together to bring to Colombia his successful Argentinian pharmacy chain. He enthusiastically proposed, "I put up the funds and the know-how we've developed in Argentina, and you start the business in Colombia. What do you think?" I was stunned to the point where I considered the possibility that I, or him, had had a drink too many.

My suspicions proved to be groundless when his assistant called me from Buenos Aires a few days later to organize my discovery trip to Argentina, an invitation I accepted without hesitation. I was blown away both by the beauty of Buenos Aires and by how interesting a retail business could be. It had never even crossed my mind to work in the retail sector, but I was willing to learn and work as hard as possible to take advantage of this fateful opportunity.

I had an intense week during which I visited several locations, participated in the opening of a new one, and was educated about logistics at their distribution center. I met with the general manager and several other people on his team to understand the dynamics and the strategy of the business. On the last day, Woods bluntly asked me in his office, "Are you up to the challenge or not?" I expressed my enthusiasm and interest, but I was also transparent about my fears, as I didn't know whether or not my inexperience in the retail sector could disqualify me from heading the business in Colombia. "Don't worry! Surround yourself well, put a great team together, and I am sure it will be a success," he responded. We hammered out the logistical and economic details of the deal, and I returned to share the results of the trip with my wife.

The decision to return to Colombia wasn't easy. We had been abroad for about five years, and had enjoyed the privileges of living in a country free of conflict. The situation in Colombia was far from ideal. In 2002, more than 2500 extortion-related kidnappings were reported, and a massacre occurred somewhere every two days. Leaving the peacefulness of Switzerland for the chaos in Colombia was a bitter pill to swallow. On the other hand, we also considered the blessing of having Juan Martin grow up close to his cousins, uncles, aunts, and grandparents, and we couldn't ignore the tangible benefit of a formal job offer.

We returned, hopeful but fearful. While living abroad, we had tended to magnify the problems of our native country. While Colombia's problems are certainly noticeable when living there, they had become unrealistically daunting when viewed from the outside. At least, that's what we thought.

In early 2003, just a few weeks after our arrival, we were eating dinner at my brother's home to celebrate our return and plan new projects as a family when a bomb suddenly exploded a few blocks away, in Club El Nogal, leaving more than thirty dead and hundreds wounded. I still remember how Pilar and I looked at each other in horror; our expressions both agreed that we had made the wrong choice. When we felt the shockwave, heard the sirens of fire trucks and ambulances, and watched on television the images of what was happening a few blocks away, we understood the problem; we were living the tragedy of our country, not sitting in front of the Swiss Alps and reading about it in a newspaper. We found the experience extremely unsettling, and so did many others. "Colombia cries but does not give up," was the slogan Colombians repeated to convince themselves to continue fighting for a country filled with violence, but also with opportunity.

My former partners lent me a small office so I could begin my work. Following Woods' recommendation, I hired an executive head-hunting firm to assemble a top-notch team, a task that we accomplished successfully. We endeavored as a group to develop the strategy that was later approved by the board in Argentina, and we opened our first location just a few months after, in Bogota's iconic Centro Andino. I remember the great satisfaction I felt that night while admiring the impressive, well-lit store, replete with aisles brimming with products. Of course, what excited me the most was seeing the curious expressions on the faces of people as they walked by and entered the store to shop at the first Farmacity in the country.

It wasn't easy. We encountered an unsophisticated market with absurd norms that made it difficult to open stores in prime locations. Colombia's social security system and prescription coverage program were very different from other markets in the region, and the margin structure was unfavorable for us. We adjusted our sails to navigate those murky waters and venture forth, and I ended up working there for four years. We opened thirteen stores in Bogota in that timeframe, and the feelings of gratitude and satisfaction I had experienced during our premier opening were equally powerful at every new location. It was a wonderful experience learning about the dynamics of a retail business. However, the most rewarding benefit of all was the opportunity to work with a person like Woods Staton.

Although I eventually departed from Farmacity, I remained

a member of the board until the company was sold to the Venezuelan chain Farmatodo. I then decided to start a new venture aimed at optimizing the value chain of the country's hospitality industry, and I planned to accomplish this by partnering with group of friends and professionals to start the first Colombian company focused on food demand consolidation and brokerage. Our business case was based on the observation that no individual purchaser had enough purchasing power to achieve economies of scale. However, many of them purchased the same items: beef, chicken, rice, and fruits and vegetables, among others. Our model involved consolidating the demand of several purchasers and using the increased sales volume to obtain significant cost savings. I was able to visit an American company with a similar business model, which opened my eyes to the varied elements of the industry I'd need to take into account to achieve success.

Some friends were eager to join our project, and they contributed their capital, experience, and ideas. But it was a difficult beginning. The purchasers we contacted loved the concept, but they wanted us to establish deals with suppliers before signing on. The suppliers were eager to sign up – once we had deals with purchasers lined up. This catch-22 complicated our operations, but we were determined not to let this impasse stop us. We decided to propose two specific programs that would act as a proof of concept for both buyers and sellers. One program for the egg market involved a volume of eight million eggs per month, and another one, focused on fruits and vegetables, generated savings of up to twelve percent for buyers. We slowly accumulated trust with both ends of the value chain, and we began to introduce new negotiation programs. However, our business model represented a paradigm shift, particularly for the buyers. Although we had expected some resistance, the adoption curve was even slower than we had originally projected.

Attempting to emulate the American company we benchmarked ourselves with, we offered equity stakes to some of our largest customers, but we were unable to close any deals. Perhaps we were simply ahead of our time. Most of the major restaurant chains in Colombia are now in the hands of private equity funds and investment groups who would've been familiar and comfortable with our business model.

Consequently, we decided that we needed to find an investor significant enough to provide our company with the necessary capital to fund a countrywide salesforce, new IT infrastructure, and working capital. This level of backing would provide financial stability while we increased our sales volume to a profitable level. A difficult goal to be sure in a country with a virtually non-existent venture capital market, but we were able to find several interested parties thanks to our hard work and the breadth of our contact network. We had the good fortune of discovering an investment fund in Medellin that was associated with the Antioquia Industrial Group, as they were looking to invest in start-ups with high growth potential.

Wanting to strike while the iron was hot, we submitted our business plan, financial projections, and capitalization requirements. After several months of conversations, presentations, and meetings, we received the excellent news that the investment fund in Medellin had agreed to inject the capital we needed. It was impossible to hide the pride and joy we felt from our success. I popped the champagne, toasted, and celebrated with the founding partners. Our relief was natural, considering our business model had just won a vote of confidence, with the financial backing to match. We then had to go through the usual process of audits, due diligence, negotiations, and other contractual activities. We finally reached a final agreement, and all that was left was to sign on the dotted line.

However, a popular refrain in my country is "the bread is burnt at the door of the oven." And it burnt. We were left empty-handed when the deal fell through at the last minute due to a contractual issue. I still can't find the right words to express the feelings of frustration, despair, pain, shame, and humiliation I experienced at the time. It was arguably the most difficult moment of my professional life. I had never before felt so defeated. I felt like a loser, and I couldn't forgive myself for betraying my wife's trust and unconditional support, including her assent to invest our savings into the business. I also felt indebted to the same partners whom I had been celebrating with only months before. In hindsight, I realize that despite intellectually understanding at the time that all investments carry risk, I was not emotionally prepared for the result. I sunk into a depression, and I couldn't help dwelling on the fact that we'd be facing overwhelming odds without an injection of capital. My determination was continually battered by the harsh reality in which I had found myself.

Months went by before I was able to accept what had happened. I made peace with my situation by realistically taking stock and planning out what I needed to do moving forward. My partners and I made a joint decision to liquidate the company. On a more personal level, I knew I needed a new job so I could provide for my family. As a temporary solution, I committed myself to creating a motivational program that would collect the lessons I had learned and teach them to others. I christened this presentation "Attitude E," which eventually evolved into this very book, albeit after being refined by over a hundred presentations, both in Colombia and abroad. When I think about the circuitous route I took to get here, I have no choice but to laugh.

Thanks to the guidance of my good friend Santiago Zapata, founder and CEO od Hi-Cue Speakers, the leading speakers bureau in Latin America, I started delivering my message to several of his clients. What had started as a temporary project began to gain momentum. I was achieving the goals I had set for myself, and excellent word-of-mouth enabled me to deliver my keynote to new audiences.

After working as an international speaker for a year, I was offered the position of president of the Colombian subsidiary of Compass Group, a British company. It was not an easy decision, but I realized that I was being offered a great opportunity. Compass Group was a large multi-national company, present in fifty countries, with 500,000 employees and annual revenue of almost twenty-five billion dollars. Their Colombian operation had 2500 employees, and revenue that placed the company within the top two hundred of the country. Complementing my professional experience with this position seemed to be a logical step forward in my career. Additionally, the generous financial compensation was welcomed, considering all I had just gone through.

My experience at Compass Group was fascinating. The challenge my managers set for me was to double our Colombian business, which we were able to achieve within three years thanks to a team of wonderful, committed, and dedicated people who were able to open their minds and accompany me in a journey of transformation and growth.

I made sure to infuse the Attitude E mindset into my work. Thanks to this entrepreneurial spirit, we started an expansion project to get new clients for our main business, as well as creating a new business unit – which should be considered an entrepreneurial initiative within the context of a corporation – to expand the business with a line of complementary services. Once we met certain sales and quality milestones, we acquired a leading company in its field to consolidate our position. We executed a technological transformation to gain a greater visibility into the business, and we used this knowledge to become closer to our customers, users, and suppliers. We also established a culture of safety while encouraging all employees to constantly strive for excellence.

However, after those three years, our corporate culture eventually began to extinguish my entrepreneurial spirit. Companies listed on the stock market are under constant scrutiny by analysts and shareholders, resulting in the prioritization of short-term results at the expense of long-term planning. At my company, this mindset manifested itself with the imposition of unreasonable goals and budgets, repeated battles of egos, and a lack of vision. I entered an "automatic pilot" mode that smothered my capacity to create, grow, and transform, and I slowly became institutionalized, like the inmates in my favorite movie, The Shawshank Redemption.

"Some birds aren't meant to be caged," said Red in that

same movie. And caged is how I felt. I started to contemplate leaving the company. While my heart leapt at the idea, my mind was understandably cautious. I had the security of a good monthly check and all of the other benefits associated with being a high-ranking executive at a multi-national company. I was being restrained by golden handcuffs that were obscuring what was truly important in my life.

Steve Jobs said in his commencement speech at Stanford:

When I was 17, I read a quote that said something like, "If you live each day as if it were your last, some day you will be right." This sentence has marked me so much that, from that moment on, during the last 33 years, I look in the mirror each day and ask myself, "If today were the last day of my life, would I really want to do what I am going to do today?" And if the answer turns out to be "no" over a period of several days, I know I need to do something.

I had many mornings of looking in the mirror and finding "no" as my answer.

I left Compass Group toward the end of 2014. As I have previously mentioned, it was a fascinating experience, because I had discovered both the good and bad aspects of working for that type of company. I had also grown a lot as a person and as a leader. Because of this, I have immense gratitude toward the company, my team, and every person who I worked with there. I learned a lot from all of them.

I had experienced first-hand what my professor in Switzerland, Bill George, strongly criticized about publicly-traded companies. One of his articles, published by the Wall Street Journal on December 29, 2009, which was a few months after the financial debacle caused by vast abuses in the consumer mortgage industry, describes this scenario in detail. Here is an excerpt from the article:

> *Many corporate leaders took the bait and started playing this short-term game. They joined many others who believe that the stock price of a company represents its true economic value, and that success can be measured by comparing quarterly profits to those predicted by the analysts. They believed in socially-accepted myths. As a consequence, they focus on increasing the stock price through short-term actions, or approve and implement value-reduction acquisitions that endanger the long-term competitiveness of the business... To prevent future crises, we need a new generation of leaders who recognize the flaws that are inherent in this short-term approach. These leaders must be ready and prepared for the long-term effort that is required to generate sustainable value, even at the expense of short-term results.*

Now that I have lived through it, I clearly understand his arguments and have joined him in his cause to constructively question the viability and sustainability of this short-term mindset.

I am now four years into a new chapter in my life, which began with this book and my desire to connect with everyone who chooses to embrace my message. I am now devoted full time to promote entrepreneurial mindsets and excellence through my keynotes, workshops and content and I have traveled the world sharing my message with more than one hundred thousand people. I hope there will be many more who will join.

Some of you, after reading these lines, will ask yourselves, "Why has Felipe told us this story? What does this have to do with me?"

My response is clear; everyone's life is a roller-coaster! I'm convinced that each of you, in one way or another, connected with this story based on your personal experiences. We all experience moments of excitement and moments of fear. Sometimes we climb upward, conquering new peaks, but at other times we stumble and plunge downward. There are moments of joy and excitement, but they're contrasted with moments of anxiety and fright.

I conclude that every opportunity will invariably follow this pattern. Therefore, we need to acknowledge this fact and embrace Attitude E in order to enjoy our life's journey.

I'm convinced that if you can connect with Attitude E and eventually embrace it, it will surely help you find the meaning in life I have found through my experiences. And my life will, in return, find meaning if you embrace Attitude E in your life.

I invite you to start this adventure!

CHAPTER IV

ENVISIONING

Vision and focus are the art of seeing what is invisible to others.

JONATHAN SWIFT

Every personal, professional, spiritual or familial venture starts with a vision. Visualizing what we want to achieve and articulating it in words constitute the first step in attaining it. Envisioning, the first element of the Attitude E framework, consists of being able to discover a goal that inspires us, and deconstructing the goal into a list of objectives to meet it.

If we fail to clearly define our goals, we can still go through life as opportunists, but will, most likely, fail to achieve anything on a scale commensurate with our aims, and will not be able to make use of the tremendous potential we each share. Conversely, if we have clear goals and objectives, they can provide meaning, direction, and legitimacy to the plans of the present and the future.

One of the most often quoted examples on the topic of visualizing future outcomes is from Viktor Frankl, Austrian neurologist, psychiatrist, author of Man's Search for Meaning, and creator of logotherapy, a branch of psychiatry that helps patients by focusing on obtaining meaning in their lives and overcoming their problems and frustrations by focusing on the future rather than on the past—a trait common in psychoanalysis.

After a brilliant career, Frankl was imprisoned by the Nazi regime and taken to Auschwitz, arguably the most notorious of World War II concentration camps. There, he not only had to contend with the terrible conditions, but the cruelty of his captors. He also had to witness the murders and inhuman treatment of his fellow inmates.

However, given his circumstances, this great man still managed to imagine his future as a free person buttressed by his belief that obtaining and holding on to meaning can sustain any individual even in the harshest of times. He created in his mind an image as a speaker who shared his experience in auditoriums and universities. He visualized how he dressed, how the stage lights would shine on him, the faces of people in the audience, the smell of the place, and even what he had had for breakfast that day. Through focus and determination, he tried to create a situation as real and detailed as his imagination allowed. He turned this mental exercise into his reason to fight and survive. He found evidence to demonstrate that those who survived the longest were not those who were physically strong but those who maintained a sense of control over their hostile environment and had the capacity to see themselves outside of it.

On April 27, 1945, American forces liberated the camp. By August, Frankl returned to Vienna, Austria, where he found out about the deaths of his wife and brother, who had been killed in Auschwitz. In 1946, still very much in mourning, he was appointed director of the Vienna Neurological Clinic. He ended up holding the position for over twenty-five years where he had an opportunity to travel around the world to share his experiences in conference rooms and auditoriums just as he had visualized when he was a prisoner. Later that same year, Frankl published his book Man's Search for Meaning, which has sold over ten million copies and has been translated into more than twenty-four languages.

Another excellent example of the power of Envisioning is Gaston Acurio, the famous Peruvian chef and restauranteur. His father is a well-known politician in Peru who pushed his son to follow in his footsteps. When he finished high school, Gaston was "advised" to do just that. He enrolled in university to study law. His academic performance was stellar, permitting him to transfer to the Complutense University of Madrid, where he also excelled. However, his passion still griped him leaving him feeling frustrated. He felt that his life was going in the opposite direction of where he wanted to be: a cook. It was an unusual career for a Peruvian man in 1987. Due to gender stereotypes in Peru at this time, the kitchen was seen as being the exclusive domain of women.

Acurio tells that one day, as he was reading the newspaper El Pais from Spain, he found an article that caught his attention and provided an epiphany that would later change his life. Juan Mari Arzak had written the article, Arzak was an extraordinary Spanish chef who had just obtained the third Michelin star for his restaurant, Arzak, located in San Sebastian, Spain.

These lines shattered the paradigm for the Peruvian that the kitchen was gender exclusive and, elated, he took the first chance to travel to the Basque country to pay a visit to Juan

Mari's restaurant where he spent, in one dinner, his entire monthly budget. As he tasted each exquisite dish, he closed his eyes and saw himself as a chef—his lifelong ambition. He called his parents and although they were not pleased with his decision, they relented when they witnessed his passion and dedication to his pursuit. They ultimate supported him when he enrolled at the Cordon Bleu in Paris. His words reflect his passion for his true calling:

> *That day was pivotal for me; I could have fallen into the game that the majority seem to play, accepting a destiny different from that within oneself by deciding to become a professional with economic security. But, I listened to the little voice inside: "I was not born for this and I will be a cook!"*

Gaston Acurio is now the most recognized chef in Latin America and is generally universally admired within his field not only because of the quality exhibited in his almost fifty restaurants, but also for his invaluable legacy and dedication to the craft. There are some that even say that Gaston transformed a whole country from within his very kitchen.

The power of vision is evident in the case of Gaston Acurio, but I would like to provide one additional example to demonstrate this point and provide you with the story of a true visionary.

Jesus Guerrero (Guerrero means "warrior "in Spanish) was born in Jenesano, Boyaca (Colombia). He grew up in a typical rural Colombian family. His father went into politics, but Jesus primarily worked on the farm where they grew cilantro and raised rabbits. This routine continued for some time until Jesus had an opportunity to move to Bogota, the capital, to replace a relative as an office boy in a company there. Jesus didn't know much about city life but he decided to take the opportunity. He travelled to the capital and tried to learn as much as he could from this experience. Within a brief time, he found he had earned the trust and admiration of his colleagues because of his friendliness and work ethic. In his daily rounds, he came to understand the geography of the city and the somewhat complicated address system. As a consequence, he not only was able to make deliveries on behalf of the company quickly but he also quickly realized that there was an opportunity to be reaped in the field of messenger and delivery services. These observations and ideas coupled with his determination and desire to seize this opportunity ultimately gave birth to a dream: a very large dream.

In an interview for Cromos magazine in May 2014, Jesus described his thoughts and desires in this undertaking:

> At that time, I knew I had to learn because it was the first time I came to Bogota. The minimum salary was 3500 pesos [a couple dollars], but I was paid only half of that because I was under age. Part of the reasons for creating Servientrega was that I realized that the company where I was working was not growing. That is when I said: "What am I doing here? I think I can set up my own business." And that is when I decided to start Servientrega.

Although he initially thought his job was to fill in as a temporary replacement, Jesus ended up working there for three years. As soon as he turned 18 in 1982, he offered his resignation to embark on his new venture—the one he had envisioned a few years before. That is how Servientrega began. With his severance package, he bought stationary for the company as well as five suits and ties to represent his company and to acquire contracts. In the afternoons, he wore his delivery clothes to pick up and deliver parcels. As the only employee at Servientrega he did it all, literally wearing all the hats, but with this beginning came a deeper vision and a clear idea of what he wanted to accomplish:

> *By then, I aspired to have a large company with 150 offices, a hundred vehicles, and accrued revenue of around five hundred million pesos [$161K]. That was my goal thirty years ago, but I fell short because we surpassed that target by far.*

Today, Servientrega is a conglomerate that generates 22 thousand jobs and has a revenue stream of more than one billion pesos annually. The initial vision, which seemed ambitious, to say the least, turned out to be far below the mark, it was a critical step by setting a target to reach it and even though it was surpassed, it allowed Jesus to understand that no matter how ambitious or how high a goal is set, our expectations can always be exceeded and always improved upon.

The stories of Viktor Frankl, Gaston Acurio, and Jesus Guerrero, and thousands of others can serve as inspiration and a firm reminder of the power to dream, the power to define our goals and ambitions, and the power to make their visions, through the long arduous road of hard work into a reality to achieve. To understand this concept fully, we need to acknowledge that a lot of what we see, hear, and consume, is often a consequence of someone else's vision.

When we listen to music, whether it is Beethoven's Sixth Symphony, an aria by Mozart, a bolero, a Mexican ranchera, a rock song, or any other musical piece, we experience the result of the intent and inspiration of the composer. When we savor a pasta carbonara dish, a paella, a ceviche, a hamburger, or a hot dog, we are enjoying the culinary experience of someone who, using ordinary ingredients and creativity, was able to imagine and create something that has been refined from generation to generation thanks to family recipes, cookbooks, or recipes published in digital media. On the other hand, many objects we use daily, like the toothbrush, silverware, or vehicles, exist because, at a given moment in history, someone had the insight to imagine a concept and the courage to produce it.

Individual progress, in the end, influences the progress of a collective. It originates from an individual able to define a direction, set a goal, and follow through. The ability to dream and translate a dream into concrete personal objectives is ultimately what produced geniuses like Einstein, Da Vinci or Copernicus; artists like Rembrandt, Picasso, or Dali; popular musicians like Pavarotti, Sting, Juanes, or Shakira; and architects like De Corbusier, Frank Lloyd Wright, or Renzo Piano. Throughout all disciplines, we can see how aspiration, coupled with the necessary follow through transformed an ephemeral dream into a concrete reality.

Our day-to-day affairs often result in a cyclical pattern of predictability. Having the desire to grow as individuals, to learn new things acquire a talent, maintaining the discipline necessary to meet a demanding physical goal like running a marathon or climbing Everest; embarking on new professional avenues or perhaps devoting time and resources to help others, always starts with a desire in our soul and mind that often defines our interest in realizing it. Our ability to articulate this idea, imagine it, visualize it, and focus on it with sufficient clarity is a necessary and critical component in making our dreams come alive and providing meaning in our lives.

What conditions are necessary for a vision to be sufficiently sound and achievable? What motivators are necessary for us to transform that vision into concrete goals and objectives? We cannot deny that several ideas flit across our minds every day and only a small fraction of these remain with us and even fewer of these actually come to fruition.

Given these challenges, I want to share four conditions with you that, if met, will considerably increase the likelihood of turning these missed opportunities into impactful outcomes.

What we dream about has to be connected to something that we feel passionate about.

As a species, we constantly think about ideas, observations, and promises we make to ourselves and others. From these, we have our dreams, are presented with opportunities, and long for specific outcomes. We do all of this to grow and to create meaning in our lives. Several scientific studies affirm that, on average, each person has between 20 and 50 thousand thoughts a day. Seventy percent of them, between 14 thousand and 35 thousand, are negative thoughts. These negative thoughts are the result of fixating on mistakes we make— or might make—and with the subsequent feelings of guilt that come with our fear of failure. When we think about the future, we fill ourselves with worry. We plan our lives around obstacles that we see and experience.22 Therefore, only a small part of our thoughts are focused on what is really important: the present. In it, we are geared to think about the future in a creative way as a place of potential rather than a natural state. This allows us to live the moment as a world of possibilities where we can be agents of change for ourselves and for others.

To be more aware of the present, the first thing we need to do is to become conscious of it. We need to strive to build and strengthen our habitual patterns by developing our ability to have more positive and fewer negative thoughts. Every time we catch ourselves thinking about past mistakes, we need remember they are in the past and we cannot do anything about them. Instead, try to use that time to figure out how to live in the present more intensely.

It is important to remind ourselves of the ideas and dreams we have, and align them with our talents. By so doing, we will be able to set realistic goals that are connected to the talents we possess. This exercise will help us curate our own ideas and projects, and select those that resonate with our deepest aspirations. It is only in this regard, coupled with the persistent effort of remaining positive that we are able to make the ideas and goals that we select come to fruition.

The dream must be big, ambitious, and exciting

All our dreams must pose a challenge. They need to elicit a sense of profound pride by just imagining the dream and our capability of achieving it. President John F. Kennedy, in his famous

81

speech at Rice University in Houston, Texas, on September 12, 1962, declared his dream of landing on the moon within the following decade. From the iconic address, I want to highlight this part:

Those who came before us made certain that this country rode the first waves of the industrial revolutions, the first waves of modern invention, and the first wave of nuclear power, and this generation does not intend to founder in the backwash of the coming age of space. We mean to be a part of it--we mean to lead it. For the eyes of the world now look into space, to the moon and to the planets beyond, and we have vowed that we shall not see it governed by a hostile flag of conquest, but by a banner of freedom and peace. We have vowed that we shall not see space filled with weapons of mass destruction, but with instruments of knowledge and understanding.

Yet the vows of this Nation can only be fulfilled if we in this Nation are first, and, therefore, we intend to be first. In short, our leadership in science and in industry, our hopes for peace and security, our obligations to ourselves as well as others, all require us to make this effort, to solve these mysteries, to solve them for the good of all men, and to become the world's leading space-faring nation.

We set sail on this new sea because there is new knowledge to be gained, and new rights to be won, and they must be won and used for the progress of all people. For space science, like nuclear science and all technology, has no conscience of its own. Whether it will become a force for good or ill depends on man, and only if the United States occupies a position of pre-eminence can we help decide whether this new ocean will be a sea of peace or a new terrifying theater of war. I do not say the we should or will go unprotected against the hostile misuse of space any more than we go unprotected against the hostile use of land or sea, but I do say that space can be explored and mastered without feeding the fires of war, without repeating the mistakes that man has made in extending his writ around this globe of ours.

There is no strife, no prejudice, and no national conflict in outer space as yet. Its hazards are hostile to us all. Its conquest deserves the best of all mankind, and its opportunity for peaceful cooperation many never come again. But why, some say, the moon? Why choose this as our goal? And they may well ask why climb the highest mountain? Why, 35 years ago fly the Atlantic? Why does Rice play Texas?

We choose to go to the moon. We choose to go to the moon in this decade and do the other things, not because they are easy, but because they are hard, because that goal will serve to organize and measure the best of our energies and skills, because that challenge is one that we are willing to accept, one we are unwilling to postpone, and one which we intend to win, and the others, too.

President Kennedy's message is clear: goals are not selected because they are easy but because they are hard. Any challenge assumed in any of our endeavors must make the journey to reach it worthwhile. This is the essence of a strong start. It provides us with the energy and the drive to realize the projects we decide to carry out in our life.

Steve Jobs and his partner Steve Wozniak, working out of his parents' garage in 1976 had a clear vision. They wanted to provide personal computers that would be affordable to everyone. Although today this seems a reasonable and attainable goal, forty years ago computers were bulky machines that took up entire rooms, or more, and also cost a fortune. Trying to put one of these devices in a living room or home office on a massive scale seemed not only to be a huge undertaking but was also an aspiration bordering on the impossible.

It is important that our goals and objectives are not easy. Each project or idea requires that we get organized and use not only the best skills we have to offer but also our time and energy. As Richard Branson puts it: "If your dreams don't frighten you, it is because they are too small".

Articulate the dream in clear and believable words

Only three percent of adults have goals that are specific, concise, in writing, and have an established timeline. No matter the source, the statistics show that this small percentage of people achieve, on average, ten times more results that those that are not disciplined enough to carefully plan their objectives.

When we are awake, we have an average of two thousand thoughts an hour. This forces our goals and dreams to compete with the rest of our brain activity. This will result in turning concrete, well-thought-out goals into a murky mixture of contradiction as they will be muddled by the rest of our thoughts.

This muddling of the mind doesn't make things clearer for us, all it really serves to do is leave us frustrated.

This is why we need to both articulate our dreams and goals and write them down so they are clear and specific. The clarity facilitates our ability to recall and communicate while specificity keeps them tangible and well within the realm of possibility

When Kennedy delivered his speech, many scientists at the time did not believe it was possible to put a man on the moon let alone within the next decade. But, setting a deadline made the challenge direct, the expectations and intent known, and pushed all of the participants involved in the project towards achieving the vision laid out for them.

It is important that we write down our goals and projects in a concise manner. Had Twitter existed in 1962, surely many users would have seen: "We choose to go to the moon in this decade and do the other things, not because they are easy, but because they are hard." But its brevity does little to blunt the overall message itself. These 120 characters alone could have inspired a whole nation.

Once we have our goal in writing, we need to put it in a visible place where we can see it on a daily, or even hourly, basis. It is important that each day we practice visualizing the end result and the goal accomplished. At the end of each day, we need to analyze what tasks were completed that brought us closer to the goal being achieved.

Share the dream with others

This idea is a bit contentious. Sometimes people recommend that you not share your dreams with others. Rather, you should keep them to yourself. This advice is usually given for several reasons, like the risk of misunderstanding the magnitude of the dream, which can lead people to judge us. Sometimes these judgments can incite us to be less aggressive in our aims. While some would say, myself included, to dream big, we also need to temper our dreams appropriately and some would take this concept a little too close to heart by devolving an aggressive dream into a simple one for the sake of making it too realistic.. The other reason is that some people feel that sharing it could lead to idea theft by others.

Although these are sometimes legitimate situations, I consider that sharing our dreams in a structured and organized manner can often help us to achieve them. It goes back to articulating to ourselves what we want to achieve and while it would be foolish to share our visions, bold as they may be, in a hurried or disorganized manner, it can truly be advantageous to share them as it reinforces in ourselves what exactly we want to do, strengthening it and ourselves in the process. But we can't just share them with anyone willy-nilly, we need to select the right group of people to share them with and be able to articulate them in a manner befitting their worth

Once we have been able to define, articulate, and write our dreams clearly and concisely, we should share them with those who can help us to fulfill them. This group, however, needs to be people who can support us in the process of implementation and achievement. This approach sidesteps many of the criticisms I laid out above.

This group, can provide us with the right feedback, criticism, and important questions that can help us better define our project or idea. It is a fact that most people who have achieved great things in life were rarely, if ever, alone. They knew how to collaborate and leverage the skills and input of others to help them realize their dreams and potential.

In short, based on the four conditions described above, I invite you, whenever you hear that familiar calling of your mind as it formulates that new unrealized dream to acknowledge that this vision is almost always connected to something you are passionate about. Should the opportune moment arise for you, seek out a moment of quiet and write it down. Rewrite it several times until you feel that the words adequately describe your aspirations precisely. Don't be discouraged and be bold, write something ambitious and grand. And lastly, seek out and identify people that you want to share it with, so they can accompany you in the journey of actualization.

Recently, we have hearing a lot about the law of attraction. This theory states, in general terms, that our thoughts can help shape the reality we wish when we are able to project a consistent positive attitude. The idea is that a positive attitude can help attract what we are looking for in our lives since the energy and attitude you display has an effect on what is returned to you. I think that this theory, while interesting in its own right, underestimates the necessary conditions to succeed in realizing and envisioning our dreams. So let's examine it a bit. I firmly believe in the power that attitude can provide in terms of accomplishing the objectives set for ourselves. Envisioning and attitude are fundamental and necessary elements in achieving our goals; however, I want to emphasize that the theory is insufficient in achieving the goals we set for ourselves. It can be the very healthy first step in getting what we want, but we cannot reasonably expect that everything simply happen while we rest on our laurels, waiting for them to magically come into existence. Dreams, without action, are fleeting thoughts that will do nothing but leave us frustrated and in the same situation many of us are already in. I apologize for my earnestness, but my job, as I originally mentioned in the introduction, is to help you to succeed in making your wishes into a reality, and idleness and well-wishing will do little to make it so.

Achieving a dream, any dream, requires work, it requires commitment, and it requires resolve. The other five elements of Attitude E, are predicated on our ability to envision our dreams. It is the first necessary step of many. As Joel Barker rightly says, when he affirms that a vision without action is a dream never fulfilled, "action without vision is senseless, but vision with action can transform the world.

CHAPTER V

ENERGY

Nothing great was ever achieved without energy and enthusiasm.

RALPH WALDO EMERSON

What Joel A. Barker calls action, I call energy. Energy is the second element of the Attitude E model, because defining our vision allows us to gather the energy needed to realize it. The concept of energy defines the capacity to generate motion or catalyze a transformation. In this context, it's the power to give life and motion to our dreams, and it makes it possible to transform them into something concrete and tangible. If envisioning is the process that provides structure to our dreams, then energy represents the momentum needed to achieve them. It symbolizes the effort, the work, and the discipline required to plan, execute, review, adapt, and celebrate.

Once we have taken the first step to define and articulate our dream clearly and concisely, we will then need to work to develop an action plan that will allow us to advance step-by-step to convert our desires into reality. While an aspiration may be lofty, challenging, and inspiring, the plan to attain it must be detail-oriented, contain realistic and measurable milestones, and emphasize action.

One of my favorite examples illustrating the power of going all-in to achieve our goals comes from Christopher Gardner, the inspiration for the acclaimed blockbuster movie The Pursuit of Happyness. For those who have not seen it, I especially recommend it as one of the clearest demonstrations of Attitude E.

The movie tells the story of a man with a dream who is able to use sheer effort to overcome a spiral of hardship and adversity, eventually reaching the pinnacle of success. His life was a difficult one; filled with difficulty, adversity, poverty, and scarcity. Gardner's story began when he lost his job and his wife left him and their son. They were forced to scrape by, on the streets of San Francisco during the day and desperately search for shelter at night, and their sleeping situations ranged from homeless shelters to parks to train station bathrooms.

After eventually finding a low-paying job as a medical device salesman, one day he left a meeting and came across an impeccably dressed man exiting a red Ferrari. Overcome with curiosity, Gardner approached and asked the man about his career, and he responded that he was a stockbroker. It was then and there Gardner's heart and mind illuminated his own vision of becoming a stockbroker. However, he knew well that a dream on its own is not enough. In one of his most celebrated quotes, he stated, "If you don't take the necessary steps to make your dreams come true, they are just mirages that mess with your head."

After his encounter with the man in the Ferrari, Gardner located one of the most prestigious stock brokerage firms in town, bought used books on how to become a stockbroker, and studied every night while his son slept. He also discovered the person in charge of recruiting stockbroker trainees at the firm and composed a strategy to realize his dream.

After finalizing his preparations, Gardner traveled down to the firm and waited at the entrance for the recruiter to come out. When he finally exited the building, Gardner approached him and warmly and determinedly communicated his desire to be interviewed for a trainee position. The man, full of himself, ignored Gardner and walked past him without making eye contact.

Unsatisfied by his initial failure, Gardner returned the following day with a different line, but was brushed aside again. Despite his humiliation, he returned day after day, relentlessly persisting for almost a month while receiving the same disparaging response from the recruiter. Finally, perhaps out of desperation, the stockbroker exclaimed, "All right! I expect you next Tuesday at eight o'clock for an interview." Gardner had taken the next step to fulfill his dream.

A few days before his interview, Christopher was arrested because of some unpaid parking tickets. After languishing in jail for days, he was freed on the day of the interview, mere minutes before his appointment. He left the police station running, with no time to change his clothes or shower. Like that, he showed up at the boardroom, where there were four executives in impeccable suits and ties evaluating candidates. They were astonished when they saw Gardner arrive wearing a dirty tank top, unshaven, and with the smell of someone who had spent several days in jail without a shower. If first impressions are supposed to have a significant impact on the image others form about a person, Gardner was certainly starting behind the eight ball!

However, as the interview progressed, Gardner displayed confidence, knowledgeable ideas, initiative, and humor, and he was able to overcome his disheveled, unhygienic appearance to earn an opportunity to join the firm as a trainee. During his training and probationary period, he was dedicated, focused, and hard-working. He demonstrated his initiative by daily increasing his client contact counts, outshone his fellow trainees with superior productivity stats, and avoided slacking off and taking unnecessary breaks. Gardner was eventually offered a permanent position at the firm, where he worked until taking another position at a bank. Chris' amazing success story ended with him founding his own brokerage firm, Gardner Rich & Co., which he successfully sold in 2006.

I had the fortune of meeting Chris Gardner personally some years ago when he came to Colombia to deliver one his extraordinary speeches. We went for dinner that night to the iconic restaurant Andres Carne de Res, and although the music did not allow us the in-depth conversation we would've wanted, we had a great time, and he gifted me some valuable nuggets of wisdom. Perhaps the one that had the greatest impact on me, and the one I want to share, regarded how he felt when the recruiter in the story repeatedly ignored and humiliated him. His answer, accompanied by a special gleam in his eyes, was simple but forceful. He told me, "I felt my stomach bursting with anger, but I was never going to give up. I was willing to use all my energy until I succeeded." I noted at the time that he placed special emphasis on the words "never" and "energy." This important encounter has become part of my speeches and keynotes ever since, so I've naturally included it in this book.

I would now like to travel to Santo Domingo, a town in the heart of Antioquia, Colombia, where Jhon Gomez Restrepo was born on October 27, 1917, the fifth-born of two boys and four girls. Jhon was only five years old when his father suffered an early and unexpected death. If that wasn't enough, he was forced to cope with the drowning death of his brother seven years later. These two losses had a profound impact on his life and his destiny. He witnessed how his mother, Maria, pridefully took responsibility for the family despite the deep sorrow she carried in her soul. Maria became an example for Jhon to follow because of her tirelessness, hard work, and resourcefulness. To feed and care for her children, she worked non-stop with the energy and resourcefulness typical of the paisas; she made candles, knitted ties, prepared pickle preserves, produced matchboxes, and put food on the table with the proceeds of her businesses.

Soon after his father's death, Jhon's whole family moved to Medellin. His mother began selling pandeyucas, a biscuit basked from yucca flour, in the neighborhood. As the only man of the family, Jhon was forced to drop out of school at the age of fourteen to support his family's income. His first job was as a janitor and secretary at his cousin Jaime's law office. This experience was a very educational one, but not because of the work itself. Jaime kept Jhon's workload light and assigned books for him to read, which helped him develop a profound love for reading. Among other titles, Jhon read the biographies of Napoleon, Abraham Lincoln, and the Rockefellers, all of which imprinted in him the belief that it was possible to achieve great things even in the face of adversity, and that passion, vision, and energy were fundamental factors for success. He quickly read most of the available books at the office, and he decided to look elsewhere for employment after realizing that his friends were earning more than he was.

Jhon got a job as an office boy at the Sombrereria Francesa, a local hat retailer. He was initially satisfied due to the higher wages, but would eventually spend his time developing the vision upon he would build the rest of his life. He told himself, "Office boy, no more! I am going to be an entrepreneur. I am going to get rid of poverty." And it was this path that allowed him to become the Colombian who has created more companies in the country than anyone else.

Jhon began by taking a course in accounting, and this knowledge, combined with his business savvy and vision, would allow him to plant the seed that would eventually sprout into a business empire. He realized many of the products used at that time were imported: brooms, toilet paper, and soap, among others. He decided to start a distribution business, establishing Uribe Gomez and Co. in 1938 to represent foreign companies like Scott Paper, Croydon UK, Rohm and Haas, Dow Chemical, and Philips, among others. Jhon later founded a broom factory, then Carton Colombia, and then Productos Familia, which would become the backbone of his industrial project. It originated from a joint venture with Scott Paper to build a toilet paper manufacturing plant in Colombia. Years later, when Scott Paper decided to sell off its Latin American assets, Gomez bought the company and christened it Productos Familia. The company now employs more than 4500 people throughout several Latin American countries.

Here is a passage from Semana magazine I want to highlight, published days after Gomez' death on March 15, 2014:

From then on, the creation of new companies did not stop.

In the long list of businesses we can find the traditional shoe stores Croydon and La Corona, Colombian Lighting, Sancela Sanitary Products, Plastic Foams, Panamerican Chemical Products, La Calendaria Markets, La Esperanza Gardens, and Montesacro Gardens. His remains are buried precisely in the latter cemetery since March 16.

We can now see the energy invested in the dreams of Chris Gardner and Jhon Gomez Restrepo made possible their realization, despite both starting from difficult and adverse circumstances. They demonstrate that dedicating time and passion to those activities that move our souls generates the life energy that enables both humble and great achievements. We can always do more to contribute to a better world by focusing our efforts to maximize our potential as human beings.

While I have focused on their professional lives so far, I need to add that both individuals achieved a proper work-life balance. For the two of them, both their families and the academic and moral education of their children were of heartfelt importance. Jhon Gomez Restrepo married Maria Helena Jaramillo at the age of thirty, and they ended up having five children. From an early age, he would ask them, "What are you going to do when you grow up? What will you be doing ten years from now? Where do you see yourself in the future?" He also invited them to think big and take risks in life when he exclaimed, "Dream! You must dream, because he who doesn't dream, doesn't achieve. You don't cross rivers without getting your feet wet, nor do you make tortillas without cracking eggs."

Gardner used to tell his son:

Don't let anyone tell you that you can't do something, not even me. If you have a dream, hold onto it. If you want something, go out and get it, period. You need to know that those who don't realize their dreams usually tell others they won't either.

Jhon Gomez Restrepo had already been working for twenty years on his fortieth birthday, and with spectacular results. Yet, we should remember how he was forced to leave school at the age of fourteen, which is why he then decided to take a five-year sabbatical to complete his studies. He traveled to the US, at first to finish high school, and his education eventually culminated in a degree in economics from the University of Miami when he was forty-five.

And if all of this were not enough to display the energy and persistence of this man, I need to mention that, in addition to all of his familial, academic, and business accomplishments, Gomez Restrepo was also very active in politics. He held several public positions, including council member, representative, senator, ambassador, and director of the Public Pilot Library in Medellin.

Another commonality between Gardner and Gomez was their spirituality. They sincerely believed they would not have realized their dreams without God's blessing, and they constantly looked for ways to be of assistance to neighbors, friends, strangers, and the needy. Since they had experienced poverty and hunger themselves, they always managed to be sensitive to the needs of others.

This leads me to the final point I want to convey: let us be careful not to invest all our energy solely in pursuit of career advancement. We need to balance our personal and professional lives when deciding what dreams and projects to follow. In the end, we should be investing our energy in everything that can help us realize ourselves as human beings. The key is to set our priorities correctly so we can make intelligent use of the energy we have. Bryan Dyson, the former president of Coca-Cola, clearly illustrates this concept in this excerpt from one of his speeches:

"Imagine life as a game in which you are juggling some five balls in the air. You name them – Work, Family, Health, Friends and Spirit and you're keeping all of these in the air.

You will soon understand that work is a rubber ball. If you drop it, it will bounce back. But the other four balls – Family, Health, Friends and Spirit – are made of glass. If you drop one of these, they will be irrevocably scuffed, marked, nicked, damaged or even shattered. They will never be the same.

You must understand that and strive for it. Work efficiently during office hours and leave on time. Give the required time to your family and friends. Exercise, eat, and have proper rest. And most of all: grow in your spiritual life, which is the most important, because it is eternal.

Live intensely and remember: listen before speaking, think before writing, examine before criticizing, feel before hurting, forgive before praying, earn before spending, try before giving up.

Yesterday is history, tomorrow is a mystery, and today is a gift: that is why we call it the present."

In summary, we need to intensely live our lives by using up all of our energy in the present. It would be best to have no energy left when we go to bed, so we can enjoy a good night's rest. Those nights when we continually toss and turn are evidence we did not use all our available energy that day. It's important to feel tired at the end of the day and sleep overnight to recharge, so we can then use all of our energy the next day.

Andres Camargo, a great friend of mine who is currently going through a rough time in his life, recently sent me a text from a Benedictine monk named Mamerto Menapace. Allow me to share a fragment of his writing, so full of wisdom, since it's quite relevant to my musings about the use of our energy and the meaning of fatigue:

Learn to love responsibility as an instance of growth. Work, whether paid or not, dignifies the soul and the spirit, and is good for our mental health. Now then, fatigue is seen as something negative that we should get rid of, and not as the privilege of feeling tired because we have given the best of ourselves. We came to this earth to get tired."

We generally begin our projects brimming with energy, confident and convinced we will achieve our goals. In fact, not long after we start, our energy intensifies when we see our first results, which are proof our efforts are bearing fruit. This should theoretically start a virtuous cycle where our positive results and our energy level reinforce each other.

However, when our first obstacles appear and the going gets rough, our energy levels quickly plummet down to zero, causing us to abandon our dreams. Let's look within ourselves and ask how many projects we have started, full of enthusiasm and energy. Now let us honestly examine how many of those projects we have successfully completed despite the inevitable twists and turns, and through thick and thin. Probably not many at all. Perhaps it's because we shy away from anything other than safe and serene waters, which is why now is a good time to address the third element of the Attitude E model: Endurance.

Chapter VI

Endurance

Many of mankind's greatest achievements come from tired and disheartened men and women who kept on working.

ALBERT EINSTEIN

The Sistine Chapel is one of the most admired and visited monuments in history. It represents one of Michelangelo's masterpieces. The story goes that Michelangelo was offered a mandate from Pope Julius II to paint the ceiling of the Chapel. Little did anyone know that it would become its greatest attraction. Being present in the space and having the chance to observe the grandeur of this work of such a sacred space left me with an indescribable feeling of admiration and respect towards the creator of the piece. I finally understood the words of Johann Wolfgang von Goethe, who stated in 1787: "Until you have seen the Sistine Chapel, you can have no adequate conception of what man is capable of accomplishing."

Michelangelo dedicated five years to this endeavor, half a decade of effort and hard work, during which he received hardly any recognition. It was only when it was completed in 1512 that the splendor of his work was acknowledged.

I want to invite you to reflect on this man, on the persistence of his labor, and on the enduring nature of perseverance. How many times do you think he felt like giving up? The magnanimity of such a task, the pressure, the doubt of coming up short... How many times did he have to re-inspire himself in this process? How many times did he re-think it? Without a doubt he had to keep focused on that vision during all that time but, at the same time, he was attentive to each minute detail. He clearly knew and demonstrated that "trifles make perfection, but perfection is no trifle."

All we have to do is to have a big dream. We need to get excited about it. We need to direct our work with all our energy to accomplish it, to realize it, and to encounter, sooner or later, obstacles and problems that make progress more difficult than we had ever anticipated. Attaining our goal is hard. We need to develop our ability to adapt to new conditions in the wake of ever-present difficulties.. We will face certain complications, they are inevitable. But we can also accept the impact these complications have on our plans, and exercise our ability to persevere and to rise after we have fallen, to learn from failure. These become our greatest ally in the execution of any of our projects.

When a pilot creates a flight plan before departure, he takes into account climate and weather conditions and maps the best possible route. However, once in the air, contingencies can occur: inclement weather conditions or unexpected zones of turbulence. When this occurs, the pilot and co-pilot, and air traffic controller need to make the necessary adjustments to the route and potentially change the original plans. This is to ensure the safety and wellbeing of the passengers; ultimately, it is about their safe arrival to their respective destinations. The same happens to our plans: no matter how much time we invest in preparing them and how detailed they are, when we start acting on them, we will always face situations that will force us to rethink and redefine to the way we adapt to a new reality. Sometimes we will be able to circumvent a storm, but other times we will need to face it head on and accept the consequences. The important thing is to learn from the process and to always keep moving forward.

We survive these situations, often frequently, but they can also leave us weakened or defeated. We will always prevail when we can manage these obstacles. We can avoid them with cunning and a bit of luck, which I will talk about later. But, I also recognize, no doubt, that there are other times when these challenges weaken us, especially after facing truly adverse conditions that consume a lot of energy and effort. They can leave us exhausted after such a struggle and even if we weather the storm, we often are left feeling like we don't have the strength to carry on—or at least we don't think we do. Lacking this strength leaves us with a sense of being defeated, because we were unable to overcome a specific obstacle we were facing. At that lowest point, at that moment when we feel we have failed we give up, we throw up our hands, leaving by the wayside the immense opportunity to learn from that failure or others and become better people as a result of them.

Failure is a topic that we normally avoid. We fear it, we try everything we can do to avoid it, and we do all we can to protect our children from it. On one hand, this happens because of the strong association between failure and loss: failure means loss.

Whenever we lose something: love, a job, money, an aspiration, effort, a loved one, or faith, this notion takes root and we feel despair or a profound pain. We punish ourselves for it, making the situation often worse than it needs to be. This fear of failure comes from the negative connotation that society places on failure as a concept. Society views it in a fatalistic lens considering it as a final event rather than as part of a process. For some, failure can, and should be, a tool that allows us to learn, grow, become stronger, adapt, and innovate.

It is critical to understand that failure is only one step on the road to success. Steve Jobs put it well, in his commencement address at Stanford University, when he expounded upon the concept and value of failure when he was fired from Apple, the company he himself had created:

> We had just released our finest creation —the Macintosh— a year earlier, and I had just turned 30. And then I got fired. How can you get fired from a company you started? Well, as Apple grew we hired someone who I thought was very talented to run the company with me, and for the first year or so things went well. But then our visions of the future began to diverge and eventually we had a falling out. When we did, our Board of Directors sided with him. So at 30 I was out. And very publicly out. What had been the focus of my entire adult life was gone, and it was devastating.
>
> I really didn't know what to do for a few months. I felt that I had let the previous generation of entrepreneurs down — that I had dropped the baton as it was being passed to me. I met with David Packard and Bob Noyce and tried to apologize

for screwing up so badly. I was a very public failure, and I even thought about running away from the valley.

But something slowly began to dawn on me — I still loved what I did. The turn of events at Apple had not changed that one bit. I had been rejected, but I was still in love. And so I decided to start over.

I didn't see it then, but it turned out that getting fired from Apple was the best thing that could have ever happened to me. The heaviness of being successful was replaced by the lightness of being a beginner again, less sure about everything. It freed me to enter one of the most creative periods of my life.

During the next five years, I started a company named NeXT, another company named Pixar, and fell in love with an amazing woman who would become my wife. Pixar went on to create the world's first computer animated feature film, Toy Story, and is now the most successful animation studio in the world. In a remarkable turn of events, Apple bought NeXT, I returned to Apple, and the technology we developed at NeXT is at the heart of Apple's current renaissance. And Laurene and I have a wonderful family together.

I'm pretty sure none of this would have happened if I hadn't been fired from Apple. It was awful-tasting medicine, but I guess the patient needed it. Sometimes life hits you in the head with a brick. Don't lose faith. I'm convinced that the only thing that kept me going was that I loved what I did. You've got to find what you love. And that is as true for your work as it is for your lovers.

Just like Jobs, other great people that we consider successful experienced "being hit in the head with a brick." Walt Disney was fired in 1919 from the Kansas City Start, a newspaper where he worked, because, according to the editor, "he lacked imagination and could not come up with good ideas". Steven Spielberg, motivated by a strong desire to learn, applied to the University of South California and was turned down three times, the reason being that he lacked the necessary talent to be admitted. Michael Jordan was rejected from a college basketball team because he was not tall enough. Although he was not short by any means, his height was not enough to qualify him for the team. Thomas Edison made thousands of light bulbs that did not work and when he finally made one that did, he famously said: "I have shown mankind all these ways not to make a light bulb." J. K. Rowling, author of Harry Potter, affirmed her failure had been "of epic proportions," She was going through a profound depression, her husband had left her, she was grieving her mother's death, and, to top it all off, she could not get anyone to publish her first Harry Potter book. She tried and she tried, but the only thing she found visit after visit was rejection and critical reviews of her work. Any and all the publishers were shutting their doors in her face.

The ability to rise after we fall, to recoup and fight on, is called resilience. The word comes from the Latin residio, which means to bounce, to jump back. Perhaps this is one of the most important characteristics that we need to develop as human beings, it is not only foundational for our entrepreneurial capacity, but it is essential in making our way through life. This lesson is also one that we need to pass onto our children, and reinforce it in any and all institutions of which we are a part. When we witness, or are affected by, the abandonment of our dreams, both ours and of those around us, or marriages that fall apart and all of those people who, faced with adversity, retreat into their shells refusing to come out, it becomes easy to conclude that we are a society lacking in resilience. It is vital to cultivate it, strengthen it, and promote it in ourselves, in our families, and in our professional lives.

The first thing we need to do is to understand the presence of this strength. We need to acknowledge its existence and be aware that resilience can be developed. To demonstrate this, I am going to provide you with some basic strategies. I will later share some stories of people in my life, but I am sure that you, the readers, will find others that you may have known that will serve as your own personal source of inspiration. The first thing we need to do is to think about the people we admire. We need to be cognizant of the fact that these people also have difficult moments in their lives, but that they were able to get through thanks to their resilience. Second, we should use their stories or testimonies to work on ourselves, and, by extension, on those around us. The important goal in this exercise is to be ready to face any adverse circumstance and get through it. It will not be easy but as the saying goes, "If at first you don't succeed, try, try again."

We should also not be afraid to educate to expose our children to the nature of hardship. This was something commonly done in past generations, and it is not a bad idea, by any means, to have them understand that it is necessary to fight in life. After all, if they fall when learning to ride a bike, it is not a big deal.

Overprotection, a trait so prevalent in our time, is actually very harmful for our children when they have to face the daily hardships of life as adolescents, teenagers, and, eventually, as adults.

There are many examples of resilience and perseverance. In fact, every single person from each of the stories that I have mentioned up to now, in addition to having a great vision for their life and seemingly boundless energy, are also examples of people with endurance. They have all learned to deal with adversity and have found enough strength that they did not know they had. Each of them recognized that to realize their dreams they had to keep working and fighting to reach their ideals.

Elizabeth Kübler-Ross, a psychiatrist specialized in near-death studies, wisely once said:

> The most beautiful people we have known are those who have known defeat, known suffering, known struggle, known loss, and then found their way out of those depths. These people possess an appreciation, a sensibility, and an understanding of life that fills them with compassion, gentleness, and a deep loving concern. Beautiful people don't just happen.

This reflection is the perfect segue to share the first of the two stories I mentioned. The first story is about a great friend that I am blessed to know: Jaime Ruiz Rueda: lawyer, speaker, and writer. He is a great person. He's entertaining, funny, smart, and capable. His life has been a wonderful testimony of courage, perseverance, and the capacity to deal with adversity.

Jaime was born in Bogota, with a cowboy heart and Santanderean blood (Santander is a department of Colombia and its people are known for their strong temperament). He was an excellent student, known for his intelligence and academic performance. His teachers knew he had a bright future for him because they knew his capabilities. He was appreciated and admired by relatives, teachers, and friends. When he turned seventeen, his bright future now just beginning, something happened that would change his life forever.

On the evening of September 27, 1971, the day he finished his junior of high school; after school, with the typical recklessness and irresponsibility of a teenager, he started playing with fireworks. What began as a fun game quickly ended in tragedy. In a moment of carelessness, a flask filled with powder exploded in his hands. Strangely, the explosion did not cause major burns, but he lost both hands and his left eye. He could not see out of his right eye, but, thanks to several surgical interventions, he recovered about 40% of his eyesight. This, however, was a temporary blessing, because his vision deteriorated until, in 1979, he lost it completely. The once happy and active young man became a passive recluse. His temperament sad and dour. His parents, friends, and teachers told him that it would be impossible to continue his studies, because they believed that, under the circumstances, there was no way to do it. During those initial days after the accident, Jaime felt hopeless and began to struggle to find a reason, any reason, to live.

He went from autonomy to being completely dependent. He needed help to walk, to eat, to bathe, to go to the restroom, to brush his teeth, and even to go to bed. One day, he got up out of bed with the conviction that he would be able to bathe himself and brush his teeth, and, as could be expected, when he tried to grab the soap or hold the toothbrush, he could not. He cried with frustration. But, day after day, he kept on trying until, little by little, he was able to perform these daily tasks. He learned, through sheer effort and courage, how to do the basic things that any "normal" person takes for granted: eat, grab a glass or a cup, bathe, shave, brush his teeth, and get dressed. He recalled how difficult it was to learn how to put on his socks. I still ask myself how anyone could do this without hands, but I know he can because I have sat down to eat with him and I have seen how he is able to use utensils. I have seen him drink water and make fun of his condition with a renewed sense of humor only found in someone who has accepted his condition and has moved beyond it.

During our encounters, he often talks about his life. That is how I learned that he convinced the principal at his school to allow him to return to finish his last year of high school. He developed skills that allowed him to retain everything he heard using mental summary tables and mnemonic words. He developed and perfected these techniques over time and still uses them today. Employing them, he was able to attain a level in which he was able to memorize everything he heard. I have seen him manage his schedule as well as his phone and address directory all in his mind. His mental clock is always synchronized with official time.

His dream was to become a civil engineer, but, given the circumstances and realizing it would be very difficult to practice, he decided to study Law. However, the people in charge of admissions at various universities could not understand how a person with his limitations could aspire to study a career that demanded so much in terms of reading and writing. No doubt they assumed— wrongly, of course— that someone who could not see or write was incapable of practicing as a lawyer and that any effort to do so would be fruitless. But, they didn't know his character, resolve, and, most importantly, his endurance. In short, they did not know who was before them! He tried, unsuccessfully, to be admitted into two well-known law schools. An acquaintance of his talked to him about the Catholic University of Colombia and offered to introduce him to the Secretary General, who, upon seeing his determination and the depth of his acuity, convinced the dean of the faculty of Law to give him an opportunity. This is how he was able to begin his studies into the practice of Law. But, he did not stop there. He went on to get an advanced degree in Tax Law from Rosario University.

As of this moment, Jaime has written three books (the first two as co-author): A course in Securities, in 1983; Manual of Commercial Entities, written in 1999; and Securities Manual, in 2003. He is an active trial lawyer in Colombia. He travels to the courts by himself in public transportation vehicles. His early years of work, passengers, who, upon seeing his condition, would give him alms. He told me that, in the beginning, this bothered him. He would tell them: "I am not begging!" But since it went on for some time, he decided to think: "Well, if they want to give me some money, let them!"

His professional successes though can't measure up to the beautiful marriage he has, and a wonderful daughter, who finished her Law studies at Rosario University just like her father. He is also extremely dedicated to friends, and, above all, he possesses an immense faith in God. This is how "hands free," as his friends call him, leaves us with a profound lesson about how i to overcome adversity. He serves as a compass for life. He shows us that everything is relative because, when we think about his life, our problems are small and his example inspires us to face our challenges and to grow from them.

As our common friend, Danilo Raymond, rightly says: "Each long conversation with Jaime is an experience because, since he cannot see, he does not talk about what he sees but about the essence of things. This makes the conversation completely different from those we usually have with other people.

The other case that showcases the power of endurance is the story of Derek Redmond, British athlete born in 1965, known for breaking the world record for the four-hundred-meter sprint in 1985 and also in 1987. He held this record until 1992, when the Olympic Games were held in Barcelona. He attended the games that year with the intention of breaking the record yet again and showcasing to the world his great talent and physical skills.

In the semifinal of the four-hundred-meter race in Barcelona, Redmond started running with the determination and energy that he was known for. He was doing it not just to win but also to break his own record. The 65 thousand attendees were joined by several million more who were watching the race on TV. Everyone was watching closely and witnessed when, 250 meters before the finish line, he fell to the ground with evident signs of pain: his hamstring tendon had ruptured! A first aid team arrived to tend to him while the other runners crossed the finish line. Suddenly, the audience saw Derek Redmond get up from the stretcher where they had placed him. Skipping on the unhurt leg, he started to move toward the finish line. His face clearly showed signs of profound pain. The crowd started applauding him for his courage and encouraged him to cross the goal. His father, Jim Redmond, who witnessed all this, barged through security and ran on the track to get to him and when he caught up with him, supported him and helped him cross the finish line. They crossed it together! Everyone saw Derek devastated. They saw him in terrible pain—physical as well as mental— with his father by his side, moved by his son's courage, crossing the finish line. This story was the central piece for the advertising campaigns on "Courage" from Nike, and "Celebrate Humanity," from the Olympic Committee. A deep voice would intone while the images appear: "Strength is measured in kilograms. Speed in seconds. Courage? You can't measure courage."

Often, the only certainty we have is that adversity will always be there at the moment of decision on a new venture. We will always find obstacles and complications and it is up to us to face them with determination and courage. We need to know that endurance is the attribute par excellence of the entrepreneur, the one that will help us confront the challenges we face, allow us to sail across turbulent waters, and overcome any obstacle life places in our path. We cannot forget that opportunities spring out of failure, and they give us the ability to learn, grow, improve, and shine.

A few years ago, some friends of mine had a great idea. They started looking for venture capital in the United States to establish a business, and they were fortunate enough to arrange a meeting with one of the most important funders in this sector. In the initial meeting with fund managers, after responding to the customary questions about the opportunity and the business model they were bringing to the table, they asked my friends to talk about the failures they had experienced. They were emphatic in stating that their fund did not invest in any venture that was not backed by people who had experienced failure because only through that experience would they understand how to overcome it.

That anecdote had a profound effect on me. It made me think because I have never been asked that question in any of the job interviews I have ever had with either talent searching firms or with top executives. I was never asked to list any of my failures. This story, however, allowed me to clearly see that failures have often yielded greater lessons than successes. All the adversities that I have faced have prepared me more than my victories. It is in defeat, not in glory, where I have been able to discover my true ability to lead, and the true power of my resolve. This leads me to conclude that the obstacles we encounter in life help shape us, strengthen us, and prepare us to go on living with a more mature and realistic worldview.

But, how can we strengthen our resilience? Can we teach it to our children? How? There is plenty of literature on the subject, from the works by Andrew Zolli and Marie Healy—that I highlighted earlier—in their book "Resilience, why things bounce back," to the works of Martin Seligman, the father of positive psychology, who has studied the subject in great depth. This same author, in an article written for the Harvard Business Review, talked about his experience: "Despite the fact that now I am known as the father of positive psychology, I arrived to it through a long and difficult journey, after many years studying failure and hopelessness." He has developed specific programs that study resilience in children and youth. Through his book The Resilient Child and a program he developed with the University of Pennsylvania, called PRP (Penn Resiliency Program) and another for military personnel, called CSF (Comprehensive Soldier and Family Fitness), he has created a wealth of resources on the subject.

Some of Seligman's conclusions indicate that the personal transformation that can lift us after a fall is generated when we are able to see the glass half-full rather than half-empty. When we are able to appreciate that, in spite of the circumstances, we are still alive, when we adopt a routine of appreciating the good things we have and to be grateful for them, and when we are able to seek help from family and friends and grow in spirituality, then we begin to hone our capacity to not only learn from our mistakes but to strengthen our ability to transform them from experiences once considered 'bad' into tools to plan out our future.

Consequently, the three attributes of Attitude E covered thus far: Envision, Energy, and Endurance constitute the foundation to undertake any venture in which we seek to turn a dream into a reality; however, they are insufficient to fulfill our goals. After all, Entrepreneurship is never a solo game. We do not see many cases of one individual excelling in a particular discipline without any help from others. No teacher, athlete, executive, or artist has achieved something important solely on his or her own even though it is often represented that way in popular media. We will always need others, people to join us in the pursuit of our dreams. That is precisely why we need the next attribute of the Attitude E model: Ensemble.

CHAPTER VII

ENSEMBLE

A chain is as strong as its weakest link.

I now invite you to look back into your past and recollect three of your more memorable achievements. Once you've done this, try to remember what you thought and how you felt at those times. Now, write them down on a sheet of paper and answer the following three questions for each:

- Could you have accomplished this all by yourself?
- Why?
- On a scale from 1 to 10, how much credit would you give the team you worked with for your success?

Part of the process of writing this book involved asking these questions to a wide and diverse group of people; because I did this, I can predict that the answers you wrote down are quite similar to those of the people I interviewed. They consistently and definitively expressed they would not be where they were, nor achieved in life what they had, without the help of others, and the credit they assigned to their teams never dipped below a seven out of ten.

The sample included men and women, singers, artists, actors, business people, chefs, athletes, medical doctors, philanthropists, and executives. Among the reasons they presented are the following highlights:

"We depend on people to execute ideas, refine ideas, and escalate them."

WOODS STATON

CEO of Arcos Dorados

"Despite my activity as a painter, a lone task by definition, it remains unfinished until the spectator reacts to it. And I deeply thank each person who has resonated with my work, and who, in addition, with his or her purchasing decision, has allowed my dream to continue. More than five hundred people have supported me. That is my great team. And to be able to accompany their lives with my work, to fill them with a little bit of beauty... that is my great treasure!"

DANILO ROJAS

Artist

"I would never have been able to be where I am by myself. We can only advance in any meaningful way by surrounding ourselves with people who are more intelligent than us."

LUIS JAVIER CASTRO

CEO of Mesoamerica Investments

"I never make decisions without input from the whole team. I love empowering those who work with me: they become more valuable, generate synergies, and make progress faster. I like to have 'democracy' in the organization, but I also demand a lot. When they work as a team, the captain of a ship is never alone. He has a group of people of different ranks who do their duties. The captain knows each and every member of his team, and their contributions are needed not just to move the ship, but to ensure they achieve their mission."

CATALINA ESCOBAR
President, Juanfe Foundation

"It would be impossible to achieve something by yourself. There is no creativity in selfishness. Innovation, by definition, is the work of a team."

RODRIGO NIÑO
CEO of Prodigy Network

"There is no chance I could have made it alone. Without God, family, and friends, impossible!"

NICOLÁS MERIZALDE
Founder, Life Project Addiction Center

"I could not have done it alone. My brothers have been the complement of what I have done, particularly in the industrial and commercial fields. It is critical to surround yourself with good people, and to do that, you need to be serious about personnel selection."

MARIO ESCOBAR
Founder and Chairman of the Board, Acesco

"No one arrives alone to where they are. In general, people don't understand the value of teamwork. On the one hand, because the trade seems not to require it, and on the other, because of the way people believe they need to act in order to advance. In my case, I decided in 1999 to leave the country, precisely to work with a team. The collaboration between musicians, producers, engineers and composers made the development of many projects possible, and this helped me become the type of producer I am today: a leader, but always with a team by my side."

JOSE GAVIRIA
Music producer

"I have arrived here in the company of my parents, teachers, bosses, peers, friends, and subordinates. All of them have given me opportunities, taught me, and inspired and encouraged me to start on a journey that never ends."

CARLOS IGNACIO GALLEGO
President, Nutresa Group

"It is impossible to arrive anywhere by yourself. In my case, as an artist, the key is to find a rhythm between working alone and collaborating, so that neither of these methods, in their most valuable form, are drowned out."

MAURICIO ZÁRATE
Artist

"Although my work depends on my talent, I would never have arrived where I am unless others had believed in me and

given me opportunities; unless, when working with others,
they made sure to teach me, guide me, be generous to me,
and point me in the right direction."

JORGE ENRIQUE ABELLO

Actor

It's very likely these answers resonate with your own, clearly demonstrating the importance of a good team for any entrepreneurial venture, and despite our desire to be individually recognized for our achievements. Athletes want to win medals, soccer players want to score goals, artists dream about being displayed in the most prestigious museums, pop singers aspire to Grammy awards, actors go for Oscars, salespeople want to land the biggest clients, and professionals want to earn promotions in order to advance their careers. Life presents us with daily opportunities that we need to leverage to grow, evolve, improve, and advance. However, not all of us manage to understand that, to attain these results, we need other people to complement us, encourage us, and challenge us to be better. We need people at our side who will share our dreams, and who wish to be included in our story by helping us to make them come true. We will only be able to reach – and surpass – our goals when we are able to form teams, learn to work with them, and fully exploit the power of collaboration.

How would James Rodriguez, Messi, or Ronaldo perform without the other ten players on the field? Would they be the same stars, still capable of scoring those fabulous goals? It seems unlikely. If we stop to think about it, in order to shine, they need teammates, trainers, and all manner of other people who work hard behind the scenes to enable the team's success. Our capacity to work in teams becomes a determining factor when attempting to attain our dreams.

There are endless examples extolling the power of teamwork in our collective literature. There is no shortage of inspirational sports stories where the spectacular final victory is credited as much to team cohesion as to feats of physical ability. In the field of music, the most obvious example of teamwork is the orchestra, which is incapable of achieving greatness without each and every musician contributing to the best of his or her ability. The audience will not experience the emotional connection with a virtuoso performance unless the entire ensemble is in tune and in sync. Military and political victories are also unattainable without the presence of talented and united subordinates. We can even look to nature to witness the value of teamwork, when we observe birds in flight, schools of fish, and ant colonies.

Among these examples, I would like to focus on the symphony orchestra, because I believe it best illustrates the factors to consider when forming your team. I will begin with the orchestra's potential building blocks, solo musicians, who are judged based on their talent level and skill. Mastery of an instrument is the result of a life dedicated to the acquisition of knowledge, the comprehension and implementation of methods and techniques, and the discipline to practice until the instrument becomes an extension of one's mind and body.

However, any musicians who've earned seats in an orchestra are also experts at what they do. Likewise, when we are considering potential collaborators for our projects, we need to be able to objectively gauge their areas of expertise, so we can have beside us true experts who complement us and add value to the enterprise.

An orchestra has instrument families whose sounds and characteristics complement each other in such a way that the whole generates the particular color and sound of a symphony. The strings, represented by violins, violas, cellos, and basses, have characteristics – both physical and auditory – that are different from those of brass instruments, represented by trumpets, trombones, and horns. And so it is with woodwinds, where we find clarinets, oboes, flutes, and bassoons, which have little in common with percussion instruments. The combination of their unique attributes generates the harmony and depth of sound a symphony orchestra can offer. Similarly, we need to do our best to assemble a diverse cast, because every member's unique skills can contribute "music" to our work.

Finally, there is the conductor, who is silently capable of coaxing out every musician's full potential so the group can thrive. There is no proper way for us to lead our assembled team other than with passion, because it's the only possible way to elicit everyone's best efforts and inspire teamwork that is both efficient and impactful. Another vital aspect of leadership is recognizing when to "pass the baton" to someone else, if that person is better qualified to lead the team. Self-awareness of our own strengths and limitations is as important as knowing the capabilities of our team.

I have a story that illustrates these concepts, although it is not related to an orchestra, or even to music. But I want to include it here because of its clear and powerful message. Nando Parrado and his rugby team were returning home on a flight to

Uruguay on October 13th, 1972 when they crashed at an elevation of 14,000 feet in the Andes near the Chilean and Argentinian border. Twelve passengers died on impact or soon after.

The survivors were physically and emotionally devastated by the crash, but they were determined to recover and work together in order to survive until rescue teams arrived. Of course, just remaining sane was difficult, considering the trauma they had suffered and the harsh environmental conditions in the frozen mountains. Temperatures often dipped down as low as -43 degrees Fahrenheit in the area, and it was in the midst of snow season.

One of the survivors, Roberto Canessa, assumed leadership of the group, and began preparations to prevent an even larger disaster. He proposed plans to solve their desperate issues regarding sleep, food, and drinkable water. He also assembled tools and utensils to help them endure the cold and facilitate movement over the snow, all while constantly working to keep everyone in high spirits. They managed to use a small radio to tune into a radio station and stay up-to-date with news about the rescue teams. After eight days of following the search, they listened with horror as the news announced the rescue mission had been cancelled due to the low probability of finding any survivors. To make matters worse, eight more people died a few nights later when a snow avalanche crashed into the fuselage of the plane, which was where the group had been sleeping.

The entire party naturally felt devastated after these terrible events, but it was none other than Roberto Canessa who crumpled emotionally and fell into despair. Up until that moment, he had been the pillar of morale who had managed to resourcefully and creatively lead the team and maintain the hope that they would survive their ordeal. Without his leadership, lethargy, chaos, and hopelessness began to infect the survivors, and many decided to give up and accept their inevitable deaths.

Nando Parrado reacted to fill the leadership void and ensure the group's survival, and his heroic efforts kept the situation from spiraling out of control. He made sure to micromanage every decision, from the simplest tasks to the most complex. When he felt the group's morale had recovered to the point they wouldn't collapse without his presence, he made a desperate but necessary choice. Parrado decided to take two trusted friends and search for help, as it had become clear that nobody was searching for them. Fourteen people were still alive, and he was determined to rescue them all from that frozen hell.

Ten days later – and 72 days after the accident – they had walked 55 kilometers through the snowy mountains. Suddenly, in the distance, they saw a person with a horse across a river. They tried to yell, but the combination of their weakened bodies and the noise from the running water kept their voices from reaching the man. When the stranger finally noticed them in their desperate state, he threw a stone tied to a piece of paper and a pencil across the river, and with whatever little energy he had left in him, Nando wrote:

I come from a plane that crashed in the mountains. I am from Uruguay. We have been walking for ten days. There is a wounded friend up there. There are fourteen wounded people on the plane. We need to get out of here soon and we don't know how. We have no food. We are weak. When is someone

going to look for us up there? Please, we can't even walk.
Where are we?

This message quickly made it to the right hands, and a rescue operation was quickly organized. With Nando Parrado's help, the rescue team found the fourteen survivors, who started jumping up and down and screaming with joy when the rescue helicopters arrived.

Forming teams, leading them, and gaining the acceptance of those being led are skills that anyone with an entrepreneurial attitude needs to master. Developing these skills will take you far, while ignoring them will ensure failure.

I end this chapter with some wise words from Cristiano Ronaldo about the importance of recognizing that one is part of a team: "Scoring goals creates a spectacular feeling, but what is most important for me is to make sure my team is successful. It doesn't matter who is scoring, as long as we are winning."

CHAPTER VIII

ELASTICITY

We cannot solve our problems with the same thinking we used
when we created them.

ALBERT EINSTEIN

In 1993, I met Rodrigo Niño through a common friend. We were studying at the University of the Andes and my first impression was that he was a popular guy: friendly, self-confident, and with a great sense of humor. His overflowing personality attracted others and he was always surrounded by people that admired him and considered him a leader. We got to know each other gradually and we built a great friendship that started with a few college parties and eventually solidified thanks to our common personal and professional interests.

His family had a printing business: Integra Impresores. It was located, if memory serves, in a warehouse around Calle 13 in Bogota, Colombia. His father's office was in a mezzanine and I always found him there, always attentive to all the little details of the daily operation. He helped to consolidate the company with a combination of courage and drive. As I was getting to know him, I noticed his strong desire to elevate the company and to make it grow. He wanted to bring in new customers and take the company to the next level by employing a strategy of innovation. He constantly had ideas, some quite crazy, to increase printing volume and make the most of the available capacity at the time. He shouldered his way into the editorial world and printed institutional and corporate magazines. He was always looking for new clients, so, to help him in this endeavor, he founded a communications and advertising agency with some friends, which allowed the print shop to increase its business. One day, as he was walking around the La Macarena neighborhood in Bogota, he saw a building on sale. Although his thoughts were more focused on paper than bricks, he fell in love with the architectural style of the building and, despite its dilapidated condition, he saw in it a great opportunity that would change his life forever.

He took note of the phone number in the "for sale" sign and he later called it, found out the price, and, in a few days, he paid the list price, 84 million pesos. He invited his family and friends to join him in the deal. They bought it and remodeled it. They took advantage of the beautiful architectural characteristics of the building and they later sold it at a one hundred percent return. Both Rodrigo and those who invested in it were left thirsty for more.

His appetite whetted, so Rodrigo started evaluating different opportunities in the world of real estate. By talking and asking questions, he realized there was a group of Colombians that were interested in acquiring apartments in Miami. He made some initial scouting trips to Florida and, based on his findings, he decided to move to the U.S. to pursue this dream. While working on his project he attracted the interest of Eduardo de Fortuna, owner and president of Fortune International, one of the most important real estate companies in Miami. Rodrigo was invited to join his team. This opportunity, to get to know the market and understand its dynamics served as a foundation that he built upon but, just like before in his father's mezzanine, Rodrigo's thoughts turned to new, innovative, and creative approaches to leverage the growth he saw in the real estate market. Through his ideas, he was able to visualize a potentially lucrative opportunity.

Once he had put pen to paper and created an implementation plan for these new ideas, he left Fortune and founded Prodigy Network, a firm that quickly moved from a small startup to becoming an important player in the marketing and sales of real estate around the world. He successfully promoted more than twenty-nine projects in Miami, Mexico, Panama, the Dominican Republic, and New York, one of which was the Trump SoHo Hotel.

This latter project opened up a universe of opportunities in New York City, the real estate mecca. Seizing his chance, Rodrigo moved there with his family. However, the move was ill-timed as just two years later, the real estate market bottomed out during the great recession caused by the unbridled abuse of mortgage loans by leading financial institutions. Faced with this reality, Rodrigo, ever imaginative and always determined, began looking for new opportunities in the real estate market, because he was sure that they were there even in the midst of a storm.

One day while browsing the Internet, Rodrigo came across Kickstarter, the crowd-funding platform. It offered artists and entrepreneurs a platform to finance their projects through the small contributions of an interested crowd. This methodology caught his attention and over the next several weeks he went back to the website to check on the status of different initiatives he was following. Among them, there were artist records and a development project on a new line for cell phones cases. After studying the different initiatives, he came up with the idea that this tool could perhaps be employed to allow ordinary people to invest in large-scale real estate assets. What was once the domain of large institutional investors could now be in the hands of ordinary everyday people as an investment option. Never before had anyone thought about this concept. It would certainly sound absurd to leaders in the real estate business! But often, it is the absurd ideas that turn out to be the best.

Unfortunately, the law in the United States did not permit this type of investment in real estate. It was for this reason that the best assets always ended up in the hands of large institutional investors. But what was forbidden in the States was fair game in Colombia. Colombian law permitted this arrangement through a fiduciary agreement. Rodrigo, ever mindful but unrelenting in the pursuit of his ideas, sought to test the theory, as he had done before, by returning to his country to give it a try. He structured a couple of projects using this "new formula."

Upon his return, he obtained the marketing and sales rights of BD Bacata, the first skyscraper in Bogota. In 36 months, he was able to raise 190 million dollars, not through banks or financial institutions, but from 3,950 small investors all pooling their resources to make it happen. Through this approach, he broke a world record for the largest real estate project in the world that was financed through crowd funding. This experience, and the knowledge learned from it, allowed him to discover and take advantage of additional opportunities in Bogota. Another project was in the Airport Business Hub, which he successfully financed using the same technique.

In 2012, to his great surprise and satisfaction, President Barack Obama eliminated the legal restrictions to carry out these types of operations within the United States. So Rodrigo embarked, not just with an idea, but a proven one. He returned to revolutionize, once again, the real estate market in the United States.

While I write these lines, Rodrigo has completed three projects and is now working on a fourth. The most recent project is a building in New York that is not only financed by, but is also designed by, his potential investors. By employing his thoughtful outsourcing platform, Rodrigo allows investors to suggest functional and design ideas for his, (and now their) projects. The process is simple: after the relevant teams discuss the plans, their feedback is taken into account for the final design. This final design goes to market in search of potential small investors. Often his investors cannot believe the opportunity that Rodrigo and his company has made accessible to them. Prodigy's portfolio of crowd-funding projects now surpasses one billion dollars and has investors from more than thirty-two countries and nineteen American states.

His ability to think outside the box took him to the summit. Currently, he, and his company, are the subject of various case studies in prestigious universities and his story has been published in prominent media sources around the world as a case of innovation-based success. Their conclusion is that the value of each dollar no longer depends on the amount of capital each investor has.

In 2002, when I was going through my MBA at the International Institute for Management Development in Switzerland, we studied a case about BMG, the record label, and the future of the music industry. I had a lot of interest in the music industry due to my passion for music, and this case study, motivated me to really think deeply about the subject matter. As usual, a healthy debate occurred during the class. The debate concerned different arguments and ideas about what could happen to the music industry in this pivotal moment in its transition. Despite being one of the two students in the class who had an Apple computer and no doubt the most passionate brand lover by far, my position in the debate was that surely Microsoft would become the new big player in the industry. I argued that the Windows operating system had the dominant market share on personal computing. This put them at an advantage. The large user base made it seem like Microsoft had a significant lead if they were to create a platform to commercialize music in a digital format. No other company had such potential for market dominance as Microsoft during that time. Regardless of the many theories tossed around, ironically none of the students or professors mentioned Apple as a possible relevant player.

What little faith I and my peers (and even professors) had in Apple. Apple was going through a difficult period at the time. They were hit hard and were losing more and more of their market share in personal computing. In fact, they looked lost, especially in such an aggressive and competitive market. Only a couple of years prior, Steve Jobs had returned to Apple as president and although he was embarking on the most dramatic corporate transformation, neither I nor anyone around me could see it. A few months later, after I had finished my MBA, I was in Miami visiting my in-laws Jaime and Natalia. There was a report of an announcement for a live transmission at all of the Apple stores. Steve Jobs was preparing to present a new strategy for Apple in addition to some new products. I decided to go to the Apple store at The Falls—a well-known shopping center in Miami—to watch it. I arrived early to get a good seat and watched as the store filled up with people. Everyone seemed curious to see what all the fuss was about.

With his showmanship and signature panache, Steve Jobs unveiled a new version of the iPod and his plans to launch the iTunes Store. I was stunned when he showed all the corporate logos of the different record labels that had signed distribution agreements with Apple. The simplicity of the model, and its integration with the iPod seemed revolutionary. But, it didn't end there. When he announced that iTunes would be also be available for Windows, I thought: "This guy is a genius!" He built on the external advantages of rival networks and seized an untouched opportunity. I returned home and told my wife about everything I had saw and said that we should buy Apple stock. At the time, the stock price was under one dollar. She responded: "We don't have any money after your MBA in Switzerland!" And, funny enough, she was right!

Today, after many years, I did the calculations and I know that if we had invested the cost of the MBA into Apple stock on February 2003, we would have more than 20 million dollars! I am not suggesting I am sorry about pursuing my MBA. Not in the least! It had been one of the best years of my life. It left me invaluable lessons and benefits and was an amazing learning experience. Besides, neither myself nor my wife, nor any sensible person for that matter, would have invested so much in a company that was doing so poorly at the time.

Nevertheless, It is still hard to believe that, given the situation Apple was in, Jobs and the whole company had the ability to think outside the box and to forge a path forward even in the face of skepticism from investors, analysts, and clients. Apple entered a new world, one that gave the company a second wind. "A computer company selling music?" some asked, incredulously, "It is one thing to sell computers, but it is something else entirely to sell music!" said others.

Apple has launched the iWatch, which, once again, strives to create a sea change in the area of wearable technology. What was once perceived as a static business, Watches are being re-examined as time-telling pieces or fashion accessories but rather as an opportunity for a smaller, more dynamic piece of hardware. In addition, there have also been rumors and rumblings about Apple developing an electric car. Dan Akerson, former president at General Motors, said in an interview: "Apple has no idea about what they are doing." In 2003, there were similar remarks coming from executives at record labels. The impact of the watch and Apple's potential electric car is yet to be seen and these products will also determine, with certainty, whether the creative effectiveness of Steve Jobs transcended his death.

While the examples about Rodrigo Niño and Apple are excellent, I would like to add one more. The story begins in the year 2000, in the early dawn of the Internet. We held one of our Azurian management team meetings at the Biltmore Hotel in Miami. One of the members of our advisory board was Jakob

Nielsen, an expert in usability (the science that seeks to make it easy for users understand and consume content presented in websites) and president of the Norman Nielsen Group. He was a true guru in his field. On the first day of the meeting, I had the opportunity to have breakfast with him. I saw a colorful logo that read "Google" on his shirt and, intrigued, I asked him about it. His reply: "It is a search engine we are working on that will revolutionize the notion of search engines on the web." The response seemed a bit pretentious to me because Yahoo, Excite, and Altavista dominated that world. So I asked him: "And what is different about Google compared with the existing search engines?" He smiled and responded with two words: "Transformational simplicity." I visited the site oftenly and every time I discovered one of their new products, I was amazed. One of the main highlights, for me, was the Google Art Project that allows people to browse the art collections of world museums. The second feature was Google Maps, which always makes me feel like a local in any city in the world.

Google eventually became the main search engine that is used in the world. In addition to the sheer disruptive power of their products, Google became famous for the corporate culture it created. It was always trying to attract the best talent available in the marketplace, constantly facilitating innovation, and were always aiming to maximize their productivity.

Google's unique vision coupled with its cutting edge facilities have been in the popular media for years. Their open offices, filled with light and color, are comparable to the corporate equivalent of theme parks. Workstations sit side-by-side next to gyms, spas, bowling lanes, and rest areas. Another iconic aspect of the Google culture, which I was allowed to experience, is its food. I had the opportunity to have lunch there when I worked for Compass Group, which operated the restaurants in most Google offices around the world. I had the privilege of visiting several Google offices in Mountain View, New York, Boston, London, Mexico City, Bogota, Sao Paulo, and Buenos Aires. They were all unique but the underlying theme of their design was based on the premise of creating a space that fosters creativity and innovation. I can honestly testify that in their restaurants, you will eat as well or better than the top restaurants in each city.

During one of our trips to Google, the account manager showed me a video entitled Moonshot Thinking. It summarizes the creative drive that characterizes Google, and it serves as the benchmark for the vision, entrepreneurial spirit, and out-of-the-box thinking that drives the company toward success.

Here are some excerpts from the video:

"People can set their minds to magical, seemingly impossible ideas and then through science and technology bring them to reality. And that then sets other people on fire. The other things that look impossible might be accomplishable."

"Galileo was such a hero for thinking big, and what he represents for me is both curiosity and the drive that humanity had and still has. This drive allowed him to invent the first telescope that allowed us to see the moon for the first time."

"There are so many challenges in the world that you can feel daunted and repressed by them, or you can decide to ask yourself: how might we think differently about this?"

"Everyone in the world is working on ten-percent incremental improvements. If you can be the one that delivers a tenfold improvement, you have a chance to really change things. If you want your car to run at fifty miles per gallon, you can do some adjustments to it. But if you want it to run five hundred miles on one gallon of gas, you have to start from scratch."

"You need a lot of courage and persistence. You need courage to keep trying every day, even if you aren't 100 percent sure that it will work, but you must keep trying. Have the courage to try, because that's how the greatest things have happened."

"You don't spend your time feeling bothered that you can't teleport yourself from here to Japan, because there is a part of you that thinks it's impossible. Moonshot Thinking is choosing to be bothered by that."

"Humanity's progress has been marked by a series of amazing and audacious achievements that go from the very small and personal to the grandiose. We are a species of moon shooters, and that is what is unbelievable and poetic about this. Our ambitions are a false ceiling of what we are capable of. When you find your passion, you are unstoppable. You can make amazing things happen. This has been true throughout history."

I believe in the human capacity to dare and defy convention, to always think big. There will always be crazy people that will wake up one day and say: "I think I can build a space ship." But if we are afraid of taking those big risks, we will no longer inspire people, no longer achieve great things, and no longer be positive agents of change.

This underlying philosophy is what motivates and inspires the 54 thousand Google employees everyday around the world, no matter their respective subject area. One particular highlight out of the many interesting conversations I had with Google's Director of Food Programs, Michael Bakker, was when he said:

If at Google we revolutionized the world of web search, if we are working on the development of a self-driving car, if we continue making progress in ambitious projects like Google glasses, or the contact lenses that transmit relevant health data to the cloud, why would we not be thinking with the same disruptive mentality about food? We need to find a way to change the world through food.

The profound desire to think big, bend and break limits, redefine our responses to challenges, and break paradigms, is more than just a motivational tidbit; it is a lifestyle, a worldview for those with an entrepreneurial attitude. The capacity to innovate is generated only by exercising the right mental muscle.

Nick Udall from Nowhere, a firm specialized in catalyzing innovation processes, says that "leaders today need to understand that innovation is a result of our creativity, and our creativity is a result of our awareness." He develops this idea by stating that innovation is about bringing something "new" into the world, and creativity is about bringing "novelty" into our mind. Consequently, to be creative we need to unearth qualities and particular reason-based states, which allow our creativity to flourish. To achieve this, we need to raise our level of awareness about our true capacity in order to transform it to a level we are comfortable with.

Naturally, this applies to corporate or professional environments, as I have tried to illustrate with my previous examples, but to drive the point, we need to recognize this as a lifestyle choice. By utilizing Moonshot Thinking in our personal projects, in the development and growth of our families (and each family member) and in our pursuit of finding new ways of giving meaning to our lives through our service to others, we are making it more than just a one-time fix to a difficult problem but are making that awareness into a worldview and perception that trickles down to all of the various dimensions within us.

To attain this level of awareness, we need to, according to Nowhere jargon, essentially inhale the "new" into our mind and exhale it into the world. This exhalation needs to carry itself into all our dimensions, and to this end I suggest the following three recommendations:

Challenge yourself every day

Every day, we need to develop the habit of challenging and questioning everything. This practice allows us to develop the awareness of our transformational capacity.

Asking ourselves the following questions will aid us in the process of opening our minds to explore new ways and find new answers to the common questions:

- How can we do better today what we did well yesterday?
- How can we be better spouses, better parents, and better children today?

147

- How can we make this product more useful?
- How can we improve our levels of service one hundred percent?
- How can we provide our staff with a better work environment?
- How can we help a person who needs our assistance today?

It is important that we take the time to ask ourselves these questions and others. We need to reflect on them, because, by doing this, it will open our ability and capacity to seek perfection. And while we may never reach it, we owe it to ourselves to strive for it. The way forward is to challenge ourselves to be better each day.

Restate difficult or challenging situations as questions

Normally, when we face an obstacle or challenge, we tend to assume a position or attitude towards it. It is a common practice to build sentences that describe the situation. For example:

- I am tired of my boss not taking my ideas into account!
- The weather is affecting our sales.

Without realizing it, we are constraining ourselves because these sentences confine the situation and do not allow us to see beyond the problem. By turning these sentences into questions, it opens up the possibility to explore, to generate alternatives that, eventually, will allow us to find the answer to overcome the problem. For example, we can reframe the sentences like this:

- What can I do to get my boss to take my ideas into account?
- How have I presented my ideas and what could I do to present them better?
- What can we do as a company to generate additional opportunities when the weather is unfavorable?

The traditional real estate industry wished to demonstrate that premium assets were solely the realm of institutional investing. But Rodrigo Niño asked himself: "How can I provide access to premium real estate assets to small investors?"

The music industry was trying to convince us that the digitization of music would spell the end of that business, but Steve Jobs asked himself: "How can we leverage digital music to develop a business model that is good for artists, record labels, and consumers?"

When your wife or husband, one of your children, or someone in your parish is complaining about something using a sentence that describes a situation with no apparent solution, invite him or her to restate the situation as a question and watch as the windows of the mind open to find creative and innovative solutions.

Brainstorm

We can usually find answers to some of the questions we are asking, but some situations will inevitably be harder to solve. When we are faced with a seemingly insurmountable challenge, the best approach is to use the power of collective intelligence. Invite a group of people (relatives, friends, or colleagues) to help us think through it, leverage everyone's strengths and solve it together.

Having a discussion with others often provides perspectives, opinions, and ideas that we would not come up with on our own. By employing this methodology in the creation and structuring of our ideas, we will almost always achieve better results. Thomas Keller from IDEO, an American design and innovation firm, presented seven rules for brainstorming sessions, which I consider to be both accurate and efficient:

1. Do not judge.
2. Encourage crazy ideas.
3. Build on the ideas of others.
4. Maintain focus on the topic (the question that needs to be answered).
4. Have one conversation at a time.
6. Be visual.
7. Look for quantity.

The best way to get a good idea is to have many of them! This is why it is so important to have a creative space that encourages the creation and search for ideas, especially when we are facing situations that demand thinking outside of the box, and, let's face it, this type of thinking is often called for in each of the different facets of our lives on a daily basis.

Finally, I would like to make it clear that you don't need to be a genius to innovate. All it takes is a willingness to open your eyes, look around, search for answers in uncommon places, learn from others, listen, and follow the tips I have shared with you. By doing this, you will be able to enter into a state of awareness that will lead us to great ideas while still possessing the resolve and determination to turn them from the lofty thoughts of the mind into a concrete reality destined to benefit ourselves and others.

CHAPTER IX

ENGAGEMENT

We ourselves feel that what we are doing is just a drop in the ocean. But if that drop were not in the ocean, I think the ocean would be less because of that missing drop.

MOTHER TERESA OF CALCUTTA

I've already praised Gastón Acurio as a shining example of a true entrepreneur in Chapter IV: Envisioning, but I would like to start this chapter with some more discussion of his life experiences. After Gastón completed his studies at Le Cordon Bleu in Paris, he returned to Lima and opened the now-prestigious Astrid & Gastón restaurant with his wife and partner, Astrid Gutsche. It was undoubtedly a risky bet, as Peru was in the midst of recovering from an acute economic crisis, while also dealing with the Maoist Shining Path guerrilla movement. Nevertheless, after more than twenty years of satisfied customers, Astrid & Gastón has been honored as the second-best restaurant in Latin America, and the fourteenth-best globally.

It was originally conceived as a traditional French restaurant, based on Gastón's education at Le Cordon Bleu, but it soon morphed into a restaurant offering traditional Peruvian cuisine, including some recipes that had been lost in time. However, Gastón innovated Peru's native recipes by preparing them using classical French cooking techniques and that is how the Acurios managed to conquer the palates of local and foreign diners, and their restaurant both started to lead the excellent gastronomical scene in Lima. Acurio's earlier bold decision to end his law studies had been rewarded by his fame and prestige.

His restaurant was always seated at capacity, and reservations were required weeks in advance. Famous international food critics published articles in culinary magazines praising their exquisite menu, especially the seventeen-course appetizer menu with accompanying wine pairings. His ceviches became famous, as did his "Pisco Sour," a cocktail served in high-class bars throughout the world thanks to its prestige, exquisite preparation, and the efforts of Johnny Schuler, who fought to establish a standardized fermentation process and guaranteed level of quality for pisco, as well as control its distribution, both locally and globally.

With fame came economic success and opportunities to open other restaurants, which were also successful. But there came a time when Gastón would say, "You're in a restaurant, you're cooking... but you're only feeding those people who, like you, have had good fortune in life and can afford it. Is that what you want in life? To be locked up in this restaurant, with eyes closed, and willfully blind?" These words unbearably resonated in Gastón's mind and soul, because they represented a spiritual void that was eclipsing his tremendous successes. He then decided to "open his eyes" and unearth a true treasure: the chance to serve his colleagues and his country.

Gastón knew he already possessed a platform, since he was

the host of a popular TV show where he shared his culinary secrets with his loyal audience. So he started traveling around the country looking for people and places that – through their talent, charm, and technique – represented the richness and diversity of Peruvian gastronomy. Among the talent he discovered was a street vendor who prepared a perfect ceviche, a modest establishment where an old woman cooked unparalleled anticuchos, and a young man who served delicious sandwiches. Long lines of customers would form outside of restaurants Gastón showcased the day after episodes aired, proof he could bring the success and fame to others he had already obtained for himself. He also invited chefs to appear on his studio show; all it took was an appearance for demand to spike at their restaurants. Gastón was cooking a revolution that would change the essence of Peru.

Gastón's success led him to expand his endeavors. Armed with his desire to discover the roots of the diversity of ingredients his country offered, he dedicated himself to finding not just chefs, but producers, farmers, fishermen, and artisans who had been providing for generations the ingredients and products that are the raw materials for Peruvian chefs. His activities helped awaken and energize an economy that had lain dormant for years. After realizing the informal and disorganized state of Peru's culinary sector, Gastón led the effort to establish APEGA, or the Peruvian Association of Gastronomy, to organize and develop the industry's value chain. One of APEGA's flagship initiatives was Mistura, a meeting ground for producers, chefs, and foodies that afforded them spaces to interact, learn, and network.

I had the good fortune in 2014 of attending Mistura while

being accompanied by Felipe Ossio, one of the greatest representatives of Peru's gastronomic scene. I could see how his eyes shone when he observed farmers exhibiting their produce so beautifully. He said to me, "When this food fair began, this level of presentation wasn't there. They just came, placed their produce on a table, and that was it." He was amazed by the huge variety of potatoes, sorted by color and exhibited in gorgeous baskets, peppers presented in exquisitely-labeled jars, and carefully-packed olives, all demonstrating the evolution and development of the culinary sector of the economy. The fairgrounds were situated next to the ocean, covered an area of many square meters, and served delicious hors d'oeuvre to those of us who had obtained the privilege of attending. It was there I realized the impact Gastón had made in the industry, and in Peru. It was simply dazzling.

But Gastón's achievements were only just beginning, as his efforts awakened an overflowing interest in the culinary arts. His legacy includes the establishment of many cooking schools, including some with international acclaim, where thousands of students dream of carving out a place in Peru's now-impressive culinary world. With the vision of providing the disadvantaged an opportunity to study cooking and participate in his grand movement, Gastón founded the Pachacútec Culinary School, where young people from low-income households have the opportunity to master cooking learning from Gastón and his local and international friends, who include Juan Mari Arzak and Ferran Adrià. These select students then have the chance to work at Gastón's restaurants after graduation, and they are recruited by the most prestigious restaurants around the globe.

All of these achievements are undoubtedly the result of Gastón Acurio's talent, vision, energy, endurance, ensemble, and mental elasticity. But he wouldn't have been able to properly display his skills if he hadn't decided to dedicate his life and career to a higher calling. When he opened his eyes and used his talent and ability to "engage" with others, and to toil for the benefit of his colleagues and his country, he was able to provide the opportunities so many of his compatriots now enjoy. Through them, he was able to change the identity of a nation. According to Felipe Ossio, "Gastón has changed the lives of many farmers, chefs, and business people in the restaurant sector, and that is why we love him so much." The most compelling aspect of his story is knowing that, by engaging with a cause, he now has more than fifty restaurants in fourteen countries. When prestigious writer Mario Vargas Llosa proposed Gastón as a presidential candidate, he magnificently responded, "A chef can do many good things for his country, without falling into the vanity of believing he is a savior."

When you are fortunate enough to discover and invest all of your love into your life's purpose, the ordinary can be replaced by the extraordinary. It may sound strange to discuss love in a book about entrepreneurship, but when you realize that only the loving teacher achieves greatness, that only the athlete who loves to train will win gold medals, and that the salesperson who loves to sell is the one who will sell the most, we understand that loving what we do is an entirely relevant and transformational concept.

A Bible passage from the first letter of Saint Paul to the Corinthians reads:

If I speak in the tongues of men or of angels, but do not have
love, I am only a resounding gong or a clanging cymbal. If I
have the gift of prophecy and can fathom all mysteries and
all knowledge, and if I have a faith that can move mountains,
but do not have love, I am nothing. If I give all I possess to
the poor and give over my body to hardship that I may boast,
but do not have love, I gain nothing.

Let the power of these words loudly resound within you, because they are direct and true! No matter how valuable our ideas may be, how much energy we spend on them, how many times we bounce back, how well we're supported, or how creatively and effectively we innovate, if we do not devote all of our love while working toward a higher purpose, such as serving others, we are doomed to failure!

Aristotle once said that love is to "discover, choose, and wish to realize good things for the sake of others." For Gastón Acurio, opening his eyes allowed him to work toward an improved and fascinating world where he's been able to perform good works for the sake of others, and that is the reason for the magnitude of his success. He had already achieved success with Astrid & Gastón, but how much would he have left undone had he simply remained a cook?

Engaging is empathizing by putting yourself in the shoes of others, discovering how you can help them, and pouring your efforts into achieving the greatest possible outcome. Although none of us can attain perfection, we should certainly be striving for it! Engaging is living our lives based on lofty principles and ethical values; it's never being complacent and always believing that any situation, no matter how good it may seem, can be improved.

"Mr. President, we have lowered infant mortality in Cartagena by 81 percent in seven years, and it cost us less than three hundred thousand dollars." When Catalina Escobar, Executive Director of the Juan Felipe Gomez Escobar Foundation, made this declaration during her speech for the inauguration of an impressive 130,000 square-foot housing complex in Cartagena, she received a standing ovation. The president of Colombia and his wife also clapped; however, their faces also expressed frustration, seeing that Catalina and her team had achieved in a short time what governments of Colombia had not despite decades of effort and hundreds of millions of dollars spent.

How can we explain this discrepancy? Catalina's tenacity, grit, and endurance were partially responsible, but these attributes were also present in many of the government officials who had previously tried to solve this tragic problem. The real difference lies in Catalina's engagement with her cause and the love she has put into her work. Paradoxically, this love was born out of a profound and indescribable pain.

Catalina had previously worked as a volunteer in the maternity ward at the Rafael Calvo Maternity Clinic. One afternoon, among the many she had spent there, a small infant died in her arms because his parents did not have the thirty thousand pesos (equivalent to $10) needed to pay for the treatment that could have saved his life. Catalina's pain, sadness, and frustration stabbed deeply into her being. But she was only truly able to understand what the baby's mother had felt a few weeks later, when her own eighteen-month-old child, Juan Felipe, tragically died after falling from her apartment's balcony. "I cannot let more mothers suffer such a great pain," Catalina declared to herself in the midst of her profound agony.

These tragic events led to the creation of the Juan Felipe Gomez Escobar Foundation, whose purpose has been to save the lives of at-risk children. It is not acceptable for babies to die because their parents can't pay thirty thousand pesos! Catalina accomplished her goal through dedication and effort. Her foundation built and equipped a state of the art neonatal intensive care unit (NICU) at the Rafael Calvo Maternity Clinic, and also developed the necessary control procedures that resulted in an impressive reduction in the infant mortality rate in the beautiful city of Cartagena, where luxury and opulence co-exist with misery and extreme poverty.

This gratifying journey led Catalina and her team to discover that, although the infant mortality problem was important, it was merely a symptom of a larger, more complex problem, one with serious ramifications for the city and the country. They detected that a high percentage of the babies born at the clinic – a representative sample, because half of the babies in Cartagena are born there – were birthed by unwed mothers, and underage, unwed mothers in particular. The effects of having pregnant girls as young as eleven and twelve years old are disastrous for society. Every one of these new mothers are forced to interrupt their education and dreams to unpreparedly confront motherhood. Their living conditions are almost always shockingly unacceptable, and many of them end up with multiple pregnancies. The resulting low educational levels of these mothers limits their capacity to work, perpetuating a vicious cycle of poverty. After this sobering statistical picture became evident to the foundation, they decided to branch out and tackle this issue alongside their original raison d'être.

The foundation subsequently set up three programs that have produced stunning results: (1) more than 2500 adolescent first-time mothers have been trained in a productive trade, seventy percent have returned to the educational system, and ninety percent are in good health; (2) follow-up visits with adolescent mothers, which have resulted in seventy percent of participants earning a stable income, and ninety-five percent avoiding another unplanned pregnancy; (3) the Office of Employment and Entrepreneurship, whose mission is to match the adolescent mothers trained by the foundation with the city's job opportunities. In addition, the office makes sure the young women have proper, legally-compliant working conditions. The results of all three programs have been so outstanding that experts have declared that, through her foundation, Catalina has developed a model to break poverty cycles. Her programs and processes have not only received numerous national and international awards, but have also provided a case study for governments, universities, and foundations around the world that seek to replicate her results in other areas with similar challenges.

While visiting the foundation's headquarters will certainly showcase Catalina's ability to inspire her team, a greater impact will be felt by witnessing her relationship with the girls who benefit from her programs, as well as the healthy environment that allows their babies to laugh, play, and experience life with the dignity that all human beings deserve while their mothers receive training. Hugs, kisses, and gestures of gratitude and affection are everywhere. It's in the shiny eyes of these girls and their small children that you can see a reflection of the love, dedication, and engagement that have allowed this program to flourish as it has.

Consequently, we must find a higher purpose beyond what we endeavor to accomplish, with the ultimate end of discovering how our efforts can serve others. If we opt to get married, let us do it to serve and make our spouse happy; if we want children, let it be to love them and dedicate our lives to them; if we decide to study, let us do it to employ our knowledge for the good of others; if we want to be promoted at work, let us be motivated to use our efforts, skills, and dedication to serve the company and its customers; and, lastly, if we decide to start a new business, let us do it to provide tangible benefits for our future employees and customers.

Finding purpose will make our journey easier, will encourage us in moments of adversity and uncertainty, and will always provide meaning to our lives. Let us do everything with boundless love because...

Intelligence without love is malevolent.
Justice without love is heartless.
Diplomacy without love is hypocrisy.
Success without love is arrogance.
Wealth without love is avarice.
Docility without love is servitude.
Poverty without love is conceit.
Truth without love is hurtful.
Authority without love is tyranny.

Work without love is slavery.
Simplicity without love degrades.
Prayer without love isolates.
Law without love is oppression.
Faith without love is fanaticism.
Life without love is meaningless.

-MOTHER TERESA OF CALCUTTA

CHAPTER X

SERENDIPITY

Diligence is the mother of good fortune.

BENJAMIN DISRAELI

From the beginning of this book, I have been mentioning that there are six attributes of Attitude E. In previous chapters we delved into each of them in detail and, I have some news for you...I want to introduce a new one, a seventh attribute, in this chapter: sErendipity.

I have kept this particular attribute separate because it is the only one we cannot control. We all have the power and the will to decide if we want to dream. In dreaming, we decide if we want to envision a new reality for ourselves. We all have the opportunity to put our energy into the things we care about. We can give up or persevere when we face adversity. We can choose to improve our ability to endure difficult situations come what may. We can opt to work alone or to surround ourselves with an ensemble of people who complement and enrich us. By doing so, we ultimately discover the power of a team. We can have a closed vision of the world or we can open our minds to think outside the box. We should always approach problems with imagination and strive to find new answers to the questions we face. By utilizing the elasticity of our minds, we can overcome so many different obstacles that we never thought possible. And, finally, we can achieve our goals selfishly, thinking about ourselves, or engage things with a larger purpose in mind. By focusing on serving others we not only serve them but serve ourselves in the process. The last factor is unpredictable and resides outside of our control. I have called it serendipity before, because the term seems to represent moments when we experience good fortune, inexplicable gifts from life itself. What many of us call gifts from God and others describe as the luck factor can play a determining role in our lives. A great friend and boss, Jacky Goldstein, said it well. We were enjoying a glass of wine in Santo Domingo square in Cartagena in 2001 when he said: "Life is determined by low-probability events."

In 1994, when I lived in London, I was able to enjoy the incredible concerts the city offers. Every day, there were countless concerts and the only seeming limitation was having the sufficient means to attend them. As I was there as a student, I was looking for whatever was affordable—without sacrificing quality, of course. There were weeks when I was able to attend up to five concerts, but I did manage to go to at least three a week. Every Wednesday, I spent a great deal of time evaluating the program that was published in the newest edition of Time Out magazine.

I remember on a Wednesday in April, I couldn't believe my eyes when I saw the night's offering. At 7pm, the London Philharmonic was performing at St. Paul's Cathedral. It was a concert to pay homage to Andrew Lloyd Webber, composer of many musicals such as: Cats, Phantom of the Opera, Starlight Express, and Evita, among others. I would like to say that musical theater was—at the time—one of my favorite genres and Andrew Lloyd Webber was arguably one of its greatest representatives. The concert, suffice to say, was in my list of must-sees, and seeing him live would mean a lot to me. To top it all off, the fact that the London Philharmonic would be performing his music not to mention the venue was St. Paul's Cathedral were icing on the cake. I could not miss it for the world!

Without thinking twice, I took the tube to try to arrive on time and buy the tickets. I learned before that concerts in churches were often free or, typically, very inexpensive. I did not have any reason to suspect that this concert would be any different. When I arrived to the cathedral and queued up in line to enter, I found myself before the ticket table. When my turn came, a British girl explained that this was a benefit concert to collect funds to repair the dome of the cathedral and the least expensive ticket was three hundred pounds sterling! I do not know if it was my face, but I could see how she looked at me and I am sure my face had expressed frustration and pain.

I knew I could not afford it. I turned around and left the cathedral with my head down. I was slowly going down the stairs and when I got to the last step, I thought: "When else am I going to have this opportunity again in my life?" Maybe motivated by this idea or simply by the overwhelming desire to go in, I turned around and decided to pay the three hundred pounds, which was the cost of two weeks at the YMCA boarding house where I was living in London.

I made it back to the table and the same girl smiled at me and said: "You're back! How about paying only twenty pounds?"

Surprised, I answered: "Sounds great!" I handed her a twenty-pound bill and she gave me a ticket. She called the usher and said: "Accompany this gentleman to his seat." "Follow me," said the man, and he guided me along the central aisle of the magnificent cathedral. He reached a place where there was a chained off area that was clearly set aside for a new "category" of attendees. I was surprised when he unhooked the chain, looked at me, and said: "This way." We continued walking and then I saw the enormous and beautiful dome. The iconic dome of this great architectural marvel, inexplicably survived the Nazi attacks during World War II and here I was standing below it. We were gathered there that evening, joined in a fundraising effort for its restoration. There were countless automated spotlights each exuding a panoply of color that lit the space and made the magic of the sacred space come alive with a festive spirit.

Distracted by the scene, I had not realized how far I had gone and, suddenly, the usher's voice brought me back to reality when he declared: "This is your seat." What a surprise! My seat was in the second row of the cathedral next to the central aisle. The conductor's podium was no more than a stone's throw from my seat. As I sat down, the musicians began filing in to take their seats. The only empty row was the one right in front, the first row. I even thought that if no one else came, I would move there.

The oboe began to play an impeccable A at 440 Hz. This serves as the standard guide for tuning an orchestra to perfection. Then the first violin and the conductor made their grand entrance and the latter bowed respectfully and prepared us for what would be an incredible event. He turned around and the orchestra started playing the first notes of God Save the Queen: the hymn of England, which I knew by heart because during many years, on Mondays, I sang it with my schoolmates at the Anglo Colombian School in Bogota. I noticed that the people around me started to look backward, and my gaze followed their own to settle on none other than Her Majesty Elizabeth II, Queen of England, entering the cathedral along the center aisle, escorted by—what I assumed to be—members of English royalty, judging from their attire and decor. I understood then who was expected in the first row, so my plan to sit there was thwarted.

This is the story of an unforgettable concert where I was able to sit behind the Queen of England. That evening, besides the wonderful music and the sight of the impressive venue, I was also able to smell the perfume used by a queen. But the ultimate lesson was I learned that there are moments of good fortune that life gives us without even thinking. It is important to be cognizant of them and appreciate them for what they are. Malcolm Gladwell, in his book Outliers, analyzes why some people are capable of outstanding feats while others meander mainly through mediocrity. In the first chapter, he talks about the role of opportunity and luck in individual success. He identifies several random factors, like the month of the year or the geographic location where we are born and concludes that these trivial facts can often determine whether luck will strike or remain elusive in our lives.

The people who stand before kings may look like they did it all by themselves. But in fact they are invariably the beneficiaries of hidden advantages and extraordinary opportunities and cultural legacies that allow them to learn, work hard, and make sense of the world in ways others cannot. We all know that successful people are the product of hard work and dedication. But do we know enough about the sun that warmed them, the land on which they put down their roots, and the rabbits and lumberjacks they were lucky enough to avoid?

Gladwell makes a detailed analysis of the great hockey players in Canada and he argues, based on facts and data, how the stars of the team were those born during the first months of the year. It seems that this minute detail happens frequently because January 1 is the cutoff date for player selection. Additionally, he claims that "a boy who turns ten years of age on January 2 will be playing the same sport with kids that will turn ten at the end of the year. This little detail at this age, especially during pre-adolescence, makes a considerable difference in physical maturity." He then turns his attention, in a similar fashion, to baseball players. He found that they are often children of high academic achievement that even carries over into the university. In all cases, successful individuals possessed a special talent, but they also had an advantage, an opportunity they neither deserved nor earned.

Besides those fortuitous factors, which Gladwell describes in detail in his book, there are also moments when the stars simply align in our favor. Some years ago, during a family trip to Chicago, I had the fortune of listening to Tchaikovsky's 1812 Overture performed by the Chicago Symphony at the Ravinia Festival on the outskirts of the city. The public was sitting on the lawn in a beautiful park. We enjoyed the event with the whole family, and the picnic we had was amazing, courtesy of my childhood friend Luis Jorge Zapp. Before the concert began, I took the program and leafed through it. There, I found an intriguing story. It was entitled "When dreams come true," written by the piano virtuoso Lang Lang.

He wrote how, in 1999, the famous German pianist Andre Watts had to cancel his participation in one of the main concerts at the Ravinia Festival for health reasons. That same day, Lang Lang, received a call from his manager who excitedly informed him that the organizers of the festival wanted him to be Watts' replacement to play that evening Tchaikovsky's Concerto No. 1 for piano and orchestra. "You have to be at the airport in ninety minutes," said his manager. Lang Lang was blown away and could not even say a word.

He took the flight from New York and arrived in Chicago. He was able to rehearse with the orchestra for couple of hours and waited thrilled until the third bell announced the start of the concert. He mentions that he recalled the conductor saying to him: "We have been practicing this with Andre for several weeks, but now it seems we have also done it with you." Lang Lang felt the same way. He sensed his hands floating across the keys and he was aware of how his notes complemented the orchestra with total synchronicity. In his own words:

Just a few days back I was reading about the Gala of the Century in a magazine, imagining the thrill of playing with the Chicago Symphony, a thrill that, according to what those who knew the competitive world of music had told me, could happen in about ten years. On that day, the thrill was mine. I was in the dressing room putting on my concert attire, and with the partially open door, I could hear Leon Fleisher playing Brahms. My time had arrived...

The audience was expecting Andre Watts, but Isaac Stern, violin virtuoso and festival organizer announced that, due to health reasons, the German pianist had been unable to attend but he promised the audience they would not forget what they were about to hear. He talked about a young prodigy from China who, at only seventeen years of age, would give people plenty to talk about. This is how Lang Lang put it:

> *When I played the last note, there was a silence that bridged to an explosion. One of the critics who witnessed this superb event described it as an "electric charge." I looked at the audience and I saw thousands of people standing up, applauding with enthusiasm. It was the best moment of my life. In my heart I knew it was the beginning of something new, of a new life for me.*

I am in no way casting doubt on Lang Lang's talent, practice or his discipline, but it is important to recognize the magnitude of this moment and possibility that life gave him. This event, which occurred thanks to a stroke of luck or a blessing from God—as I clearly see it—accelerated his journey to fame and catapulted him to be recognized as one of the great classical pianists in the world today.

In the speech that Woods Staton delivered at my graduation ceremony at IMD in Switzerland, which I alluded to back in the introduction to this book, he spoke about the role of luck in success. What a coincidence! Again, I would like to point out that, in that moment of my life, it was he who defined my professional future.

I quote him:

The final key to success is to be alert to moments of seren-dipity. I believe there is a lot an individual can do to develop a career, but success is often somewhat accidental. Much depends on being in the right place at the right time but also on recognizing that you're in the right place at the right time, being alert to opportunities and taking advantage of the good fortune that comes your way. Of the six success factors I've outlined, serendipity is obviously the least possible to con-trol. You certainly can't control what luck comes your way, but you can and should make every effort to convert luck into opportunity.

A concrete example I'd like to offer goes back to my job search after I left Panamco and it illustrates the importance of converting luck to opportunity. Almost a year after I left Panamco, I learned of a position as Operations Director for the Colombian airline Aces. I flew into Medellin for an early morning meeting with the President of the company. When I arrived, his secretary told me the President had an emergen-cy and needed to cancel the meeting. Left with disappoint-ment and some free time, I contacted a friend who invited me to lunch. This friend startled me by asking: "Why are you looking for a job? Why don't you set up something on your own?" I replied that I couldn't think of a business to run. My friend told me he knew some people who wanted to set up a McDonald's franchise in Colombia and needed an operations manager. He suggested I meet with them. Eventually, on *behalf of these individuals, I began negotiations with McDonald's. The situation became delicate when McDonald's told me they would work only with active investor/managers. I approached my partners and asked to be released from our agreement. Happily for me, they agreed and I was freed to negotiate my own terms with McDonald's. Ultimately, we were not able to enter Colombia because of political difficulties. McDonald's asked me to prepare plans to enter Argentina instead. Sixteen years later, I am the Joint Venture Partner of McDonald's in Argentina, and head the operations in Argentina, Chile, Uruguay, and Paraguay, with a total of over 300 restaurants and sales of $400,000,000. Needless to say, I have never again thought about the airline business – other than as a frequent passenger! My career and, indeed, my life probably would have developed very differently if my meeting with the president of the airline in 1982 had not been canceled. My career has been shaped by a series of small accidents, and by my ability to convert unexpected opportunities into productive new avenues."*

Today, thirteen years after that speech, Woods Staton owns McDonalds' master franchise for all of Latin America. They have over three thousand restaurants, around one hundred thousand employees, and he is now on Forbes billionaire list. I know him well and I can testify about his impressive management skills and his capacity to lead. I am convinced that 99 percent of his success is due to these attributes. However, it is worthwhile to ask ourselves how much weight that fortuitous event in Medellin had. Perhaps it was one percent, but it was pivotal for his success!

Good fortune not only applies to individuals; the enterprise world is also full of examples that demonstrate that luck allowed many companies to go to market with unplanned products that later became pillars of their success. Some generic examples are the microwave oven, fireworks, and modeling clay, which were discovered by accident because companies were actually looking for a new technology for radars, a new cooking technique, and a new wall cleaner.

Other examples are 3M's Post-It notes and their arsenal of related products. It was created by Arthur Fry, starting with a new adhesive that was accidentally developed in the company labs when they were looking for a completely different application. Another case involves Pfizer, a pharmaceutical company that invested millions of dollars and years of clinical trials for a medication that promised a cure for blood pressure disorders. During the trials, they found out that it was not effective for the original purpose, but they found an unforeseen side effect that led Pfizer to create Viagra, one the company's most successful drugs. I really admire their commercial vision, since it would have been easier to accept that the drug simply did not work for its intended purpose and continue the search for new drugs in their Research and Development process.

To conclude, it is important for me to clarify that it is not my intension to say that those who assume an entrepreneurial attitude have better luck than others. I am convinced that we are all blessed with wonderful opportunities that impact our lives and the important thing is to be cognizant, recognize them, and take full advantage of opportunities that come our way. On the other hand, I am convinced that people with an entrepreneurial attitude are always attentive and vigilant. They are able to see when those opportunities arise and they try to turn these serendipitous occasions into constructive situations that generate progress in their lives.

When I talk about this topic in my speeches, I compare those opportunities that appear in our lives to a train that stops right in front of us, opens its doors for us, and invites us to come aboard. Most of the time, we do not even see the train because we are too busy complaining and worrying about less important matters. Other times, we see the train, but are hesitant in our choice to board it, we often find ourselves doubting: "Should I go aboard, or perhaps not?" When this is said in our mind when we are confronted by a great opportunity, we say it with apprehension. In the midst of our indecision and doubt, the train closes its doors and departs, and that train will never come again. Others will come, but this particular opportunity is lost forever. I really think that the best way to confront this situation is to climb on the train without thinking twice. Like Lang Lang, who did not have any doubts about getting on the plane that would take him to Chicago to realize one of the most precious dreams in his life. By doing this, by seizing the day, we will be putting our best effort to turn that opportunity into a life changing moment.

What is the worst that can happen? That it will not work? As my good friend Felipe Herrera puts it: "It is better to make a fool of yourself than to do nothing." If it doesn't work, it will be an experience will leave us with valuable lessons that we can used in the ongoing journey. I invite you to do your best to find those serendipitous moments and to use your best attitude and judgments to make them work for you.

Conclusion

This final chapter is a call to action.

I have presented a simple framework, although I hope that you found it powerful. In combination with illustrative examples from my own life and that of others, I have tried to show you that the concepts of this model can be put into practice and achieve results. I trust that these stories have been or will be helpful not only to understand the concepts presented in this book but as a guide in helping you to move forward in finding and attaining what is important in your life, and to also inspire you to find it. I firmly believe in the vast entrepreneurial capacity within each of us and I know it is burning like a blaze. Use this framework to identify your dreams and work toward them without fear. Make the most of the bright and contagious power of the entrepreneur's fire, Attitude E.

Remember that it is not just about creating a business. Being an entrepreneur is discovering and living intensely. Open your eyes wide, look around you and within. Try to look at the world with a new perspective: the eyes of the entrepreneur. By doing this, you will start to see an internal and an external universe filled with possibilities with things to improve, things to build upon, or new ideas to unleash. In effect, this perspective is designed to allow you not only to do everything better but to help identify what it is that needs to be made better.

You will always miss 100 percent of the shots you don't take. I expect you to fill yourself with courage, overcome the natural fear that starting something new produces. Shoot your arrows straight and true. Jump into the void and take a chance. Remember that nothing will give you more satisfaction than the feeling of pursuing your dreams and bringing them to life. Be aware that most people are still in a state of unknowing and an unwillingness to make that leap. They are on autopilot and for this reason, they will say things and give you looks that question your efforts. They may even say that you are crazy. But if that happens, when that happens, remember the wise words that Apple used in its historic campaign "Think Different."

Here's to the crazy ones.
The misfits.
The rebels.
The troublemakers.
The round pegs in the square holes.
The ones who see things differently.
They're not fond of rules.
And they have no respect for the status quo.

You can quote them,
disagree with them,
glorify or vilify them.
About the only thing you can't do is ignore them.
Because they change things.
They push the human race forward.
And while some may see them as the crazy ones,
we see genius.
Because the people who are crazy enough
to think they can change the world,
are the ones who do.

It is very important to heed these words. The last three lines especially. We need to apply them almost like a daily mantra. It is not worth it to let people who think you are crazy intimidate you. After all, no one understands you as well as you do. Follow your soul, change the world, and to those who stubbornly think you are crazy, give them a copy of this book!

In February 2015 in Davos, Shimon Peres, former president of Israel, said something that I would like to share with you so you can review it frequently:

Count the number of achievements you have had in your life.
Count the number of dreams you have in your mind. If the
number of dreams exceeds your achievements, then you are
young.

Work hard, dream big, and always stand up after you fall. Dust yourself off and trudge on. Surround yourself well always. Seek out new challenges and approach them with vigor and a creative drive. Fall in love with what you do and do everything with love.

Attitude E was designed to transform and raise the bar of life. Dream, work, and never underestimate the power of your dreams. Remember the stories contained within this book and I am confident that in time, by employing these strategies, you will have many of your own to share. I look forward to hearing them and as always...

Enjoy your journey!

Eight proposals to fill the world with Attitude E

I am confident and convinced in the power of this framework. I am also confident and convinced of the results we can achieve if we can get many people: families, teams, governments and organizations to utilize the Attitude E framework. Just imagine the impact, the achievements, the dreams, the teams, the hopes, and the boundless striving...it could be a revolution where the collective power of dreaming and awareness can help transform the challenges of the everyday into a reality. The Attitude E framework can be simple but it is a profound methodology to encourage this transformation in our society.

We can be a part of this adventure. I am sure you have ideas about how to go about it and I want to thank you for joining me in this pursuit. I would like, humbly, to share eight guidelines that can jumpstart actions to help us achieve this endeavor. This is a beginning. In any such movement, beginnings start with the spreading of ideas, and you can do your bit to ensure we live surrounded by Attitude E.

1. Share everything you learned from this book with your significant other. Look at your relationship as an entrepreneurial venture. Dream and work on your relationship daily.

2. Talk to your children regularly about the attributes of Attitude E. Teach them from the time they are small to dream big, take risks, and learn that failure is not a cause for concern but a means of growth. Always learn from failure, it is our best teacher.

3. Ask your children's school what actions they are taking to forge an entrepreneurial attitude and suggest this framework.

4. In your workplace or educational institution, talk to your peers about the model and use it in collaborative spaces. View each project and each challenge as an entrepreneurial venture.

5. Share the main ideas of the framework on social networks and invite your contacts to embrace Attitude E.

6. Follow me on Twitter at @ActitudE and retweet to share with your contacts all the content you consider relevant.

7. Visit www.attitude-e.com so we enrich the page together. You can share your reactions to this book there, as well as your stories and experiences. It is a space to learn from each other.

8. Recommend or give this book to anyone who can benefit from it.

Acknowledgements

I thank God and Virgin Mary, my heavenly mother, for their guidance.

I thank all those who, in one way or another, helped or influenced the writing of this book, which was not easy. Among many things, because much of the content is based on situations and experiences I have lived, even since childhood. I will do my best not to omit anyone; however, I apologize if I perchance forget someone. Be sure I have you all in my heart.

Thank you to my wife Pilar and my children Juan Martin, Valentina, Manuel Jose, and Guadalupe, for the immense joy they have brought into my life and for the support they always give me. To my parents for all the love, dedication, and advice; to my brother and sister, for their talents and their presence. Also to Mario and Martha for their love and trust.

To Leonardo Archila at Intermedio Editores, to Jessica

Noreña and the team at the company, who believed in my work. To Marta Mendez, Estefania Sokoloff, Felipe Herrera, Mariana Londoño, for their valuable contributions to this book. To Francisco Gomez and Derek Brown for making this English translation a reality.

To those who took the time to read and proof it, thank you for having helped make it better. To Ken Blanchard, for the honor of his words for the back cover, and to Renee Broadwell for her valuable advice.

To my close friends who have been witnesses and accomplices in my madness: Chuck and Anna, Kenny and Monica, Juancho and Caro, Carcha and Pili, Albert and Cayita, Santi and Alina.

To my homonym Felipe Gomez, for his friendship and for touching my soul with his heavenly music and allowing me to be part of it. To father Jorge Obregon for his guidance and, above all, his friendship. To Lucas Perez for his brilliance and spiritual depth.

To the Emmaus gang for being my teammates in the most important and exciting endeavor: faith.

To the teachers who marked my life: Jerry Leonard, Eric Abuchar, Mauricio Rodriguez, David Gleiser, Jeannie Kahwaji, Thomas Malnight, and Bill George.

To those who introduced me to and guided me in my music endeavors: Papa Nachito, my father, Clara Lucia Sanchez, Moises Herrera, and Misi. Also to those who did the same for magic: Gustavo Lorgia, Richard Sarmiento, Jose Simhon, and the master of masters: Juan Tamariz.

To Juan Fernando Santos, my partner in dreams, to Nicolas

Dueñas and the team at Ink, for riding the roller coaster with me. We learned and had fun. Also to Jackie Goldstein, Piero di Capua, Miguel Silva, Luis Fernando Santos, David Seinjet, Nicolas Camacho, Felipe Arango, Marcus Bening, Ariel Vishnia, Pablo Ortiz, Douglas Villalobos, and Manolo Urrutia, because the journey was the reward!

To Woods Staton, teacher and friend, for his trust, his confidence in me and all the lessons I received. To Carlos Hernandez and Roberto Ortiz for their wise advice and their excellent sense of humor.

To Juan Fernando Hoyos, Marcelino and Mariano Arango, Diego Garzon, Juancho Galindo, and Andres Alvarado, for the scale of their talent and the magnitude of their friendship.

To Miguel Ramis, infinite thanks. Adriana Velasquez, Ana Bustos, Andres Bernal, Fernando Calderon, Francisco Tosso, Martha Hernandez, Jose Miguel Notario, Maria Lucia Ospina and Ashley Reid, thank you for your hard work and your trust.

To Santiago Zapata, Alina Rodriguez, and the team at Hi-Cue Speakers, many thanks.

To Juanpa Neira, my gratitude.

Made in the USA
Columbia, SC
05 March 2023

13374244R00114